The Jesus Series

What Everyone Needs to Know About Jesus

Don Stewart

TABLE OF CONTENTS

Who Is
Jesus Christ?

What is truth? (Pontius Pilate)

Jesus said, "I am the way, the truth, and the life" (John 14:6).

Jesus Christ is an historical character. There is no doubt that He actually existed. Furthermore, the evidence also demonstrates that the records that we have about Him, contained in the four gospels, are reliable and trustworthy. They prove themselves to be the only firsthand information that we possess about Jesus' life and ministry. We have documented this in our book, *Did Jesus Exist: Are The Records About Him Reliable?*

This being the case, we now go to these reliable records to discover who Jesus is.

In this book, we will examine the identity of Jesus Christ. As the most important figure in history, it is crucial that we have a correct understanding of His identity. The Bible teaches that Jesus Christ is God the Son—Second Person of the Holy Trinity. He has eternally existed with God the Father and God the Holy Spirit.

He came to earth two thousand years ago as the God-man. Although Jesus was only one Person, He had two natures—one human and one divine. In other words, He was fully human and fully God.

On earth He lived a perfect, sinless life. Therefore, He was qualified to be the sacrifice for the sins of the world. Of course, His death on Calvary's cross was not the end. Indeed, three days after His death, He rose from the dead. Jesus claimed to be the one way to reach the one God and His resurrection from the dead demonstrates that His claim is true!

Consequently, it is absolutely crucial that we have a thorough understanding of the identity of Jesus.

Is Jesus Christ A Name Or A Title?

There has been much confusion as to the name "Jesus Christ." Is it a name? A title? The simple answer is that Jesus was His name, while Christ was His title. We can make the following observations.

1. THE NAME JESUS WAS COMMON IN THE FIRST CENTURY

Jesus was a common name in the first century for a Jewish male. In fact, first century Jewish writer, Flavius Josephus, lists twelve different individuals with that name in his discussion of the history of the Jews living during that period.

Jesus was the common Greek version of the Hebrew names Joshua, Jehoshua, and Jeshua. The name means "The Lord (Yahweh) saves" or "The Lord is my help." This name stresses His humanity.

The Bible says that He was named before He was born by the angel who was sent to Joseph. Matthew records the angel saying the following.

> She [Mary] will give birth to a son, and you are to name Him Jesus, because He will save His people from their sins (Matthew 1:21 HCSB).

During His earthly life and ministry, this was the name by which the Savior was known. It is found about six hundred times in the four Gospels.

Outside of the gospels, the name Jesus is rarely used. Indeed, we only find it often in the Book of Hebrews.

HE WAS JESUS OF NAZARETH

At times, we find Jesus referred to as "Jesus of Nazareth." This would distinguish Him from others who had the same name. Indeed, He was Jesus the "carpenter" from Nazareth.

2. CHRIST IS A TITLE

The word "Christ" is the Greek equivalent of the Hebrew word for "Messiah" or "anointed one." Christ was the title given to Jesus. Therefore, He was Jesus the Christ—Jesus the Messiah. We read the following in John's gospel.

> He [Andrew] first found his brother Simon and said to him, "We have found the Messiah" (which is translated Anointed) (John 1:41 NRSV).

By saying this, they were recognizing the office, or title, of the Messiah. He was the Lord's Anointed, the Promised One.

3. EVENTUALLY CHRIST BECAME PART OF HIS NAME

It is helpful if we understand a little bit of the history of the name "Messiah" or "Christ," as well as how it developed. The Hebrew word for Messiah, as well as the Greek word for "Christ," was originally an adjective that meant, "anointed." During the Old Testament period it developed into a term meaning, "the anointed one."

Between the Old and New Testament, the word further developed into a technical term for the promised Deliverer that the Lord would one day send to His people—the Messiah, the Christ.

The four gospels, written in Greek, apply the term *christos* in this sense. The long-awaited Deliverer is the "anointed one" or, "the Christ" (the Messiah).

Later we find that Christ became part of Jesus' name. Today He is most commonly known as Jesus Christ—not Jesus the Christ.

4. HE IS NOW THE LORD JESUS CHRIST

There is also the title "Lord Jesus Christ." When the word "Lord" is added to Jesus Christ, it means, "Yahweh Jesus the Messiah." We find that it is used in the Book of Acts when explaining how Gentiles came to faith in Jesus.

> If then God gave them the same gift that he gave us when we believed in the Lord Jesus Christ, who was I that I could hinder God? (Acts 11:17 NRSV).

The word "Lord" is speaking of His deity. Indeed, it emphasizes that Jesus is God Himself.

The name Jesus, His human name, emphasizes His humanity. Christ is His title—He is the Messiah. This description of Him, the Lord Jesus Christ, is not found in the four gospels.

This briefly summarizes what the various names of Jesus mean, as well as how they developed.

SUMMARY TO QUESTION 1
IS JESUS CHRIST A NAME OR A TITLE?

Jesus Christ is both a name and a title. Jesus was a common first century name meaning, "the Lord saves." Christ, or "Christos," is the Greek form of the Hebrew word for "Messiah." Jesus is, therefore, the Messiah, or the Anointed One.

The meaning of the Hebrew word developed through time. In the Old Testament, it was originally an adjective which meant "anointed." During the period between the testaments this word took on a more technical meaning. It referred to the Messiah—the promised Deliverer whom the Lord would send to save His people Israel.

Therefore, we find that when Jesus arrived on the scene He was asked if were "the Christ—the Messiah." The title Christ eventually became part of His name. Indeed, today He is known as "Jesus Christ" rather than Jesus the Christ.

The title "Lord Jesus Christ" refers to three aspects of who He is. Lord is the personal name of the God of the Bible, Yahweh. The name Jesus emphasizes His humanity. Christ is His title, the Messiah.

This gives a brief summation of His name as well as its meaning.

QUESTION 2

Is Jesus Christ The Main Subject Of The Entire Bible?

Yes. From the testimony Jesus Himself, we find that the entire Scripture is all about Him. Indeed, He said the following to the religious leaders of His day.

> You search the Scriptures because you think that in them you have eternal life; it is these that testify about Me . . . For if you believed Moses, you would believe Me; for he wrote of Me (John 5:39,46 NRSV).

What a claim! Jesus said the Hebrew Scripture, the Old Testament, was all about Him. In fact, the entire Bible is about Him. The evidence is as follows.

1. THE OLD TESTAMENT - THE PREPARATION FOR THE CHRIST

The Old Testament was preparing the way for the Messiah, the Christ—the promised One whom God would send to save His people. Isaiah the prophet wrote of His coming.

> A voice cries out: "In the wilderness prepare the way of the LORD, make straight in the desert a highway for our God" (Isaiah 40:3 NRSV).

The entire Old Testament was looking forward to the coming of the Messiah. He would bring God's kingdom to the earth. Everything in the Old Testament Scripture was pointing toward Him.

2. THE FOUR GOSPELS - THE MANIFESTATION OF THE CHRIST

While the predicted coming of kingdom of God through the Messiah is a main theme in the Old Testament, His actual coming is the main subject of the four gospels. Indeed, we find that the gospels, Matthew, Mark, Luke and John, record the manifestation of the long-awaited Messiah—Jesus of Nazareth. He came as promised. We read in John.

> The next day John [the Baptist] saw Jesus coming toward him, and said, "Behold! The Lamb of God who takes away the sin of the world!" (John 1:29 NKJV).

As God had promised the people of Israel, the Messiah came into our world. This Jesus of Nazareth, who is God the Son, fulfilled the various predictions, which are found in the Old Testament, of the coming Deliverer.

Yet Jesus was rejected by the people of His day. Indeed, they said they did not want Him to rule over them. Though He was not guilty of any sin, He was tried, convicted and crucified. But just as He predicted, Jesus did not stay dead. Three days after His death, He rose from dead—never to die again!

3. THE BOOK OF ACTS- THE PROCLAMATION OF THE MESSAGE OF THE CHRIST

The Lord Jesus said that His death on the cross was for the purpose of taking away the sins of the world. After the death and resurrection of Jesus, His message was to go out to the entire world. The Book of Acts records the proclamation of the message of Jesus Christ. The key verse of the Book of Acts records the following words of Jesus.

> But you will receive power when the Holy Spirit has come upon you, and you will be My witnesses in Jerusalem, in all Judea and Samaria, and to the ends of the earth (Acts 1:8 HCSB).

The message of the risen Christ, who has died for the sins of the world, was to go everywhere—even to the remotest parts of the earth. The remainder of the Book of Acts reveals how that message did indeed reach people in various parts of the Roman Empire—including Rome itself.

4. THE NEW TESTAMENT LETTERS - THE EXPLANATION OF THE TWO COMINGS OF CHRIST

One of the mysteries, or sacred secrets, which was not revealed until the New Testament era, is that the Messiah would not come merely once, but rather twice. These two comings of Christ are explained in the New Testament letters. The writer to the Hebrews emphasized this important truth.

> Just as people are destined to die once, and after that to face judgment, so Christ was sacrificed once to take away the sins of many; and he will appear a second time, not to bear sin, but to bring salvation to those who are waiting for him (Hebrews 9:27,28 NIV).

The New Testament letters provide us with the explanation of Jesus' death, its meaning, and the fact that He will come again.

Again, we find that these letters are all about Him.

5. REVELATION - THE CONSUMMATION OF ALL THINGS IN CHRIST

As the Old Testament was the preparation for the Christ, the four Gospels the manifestation of the Christ, the Book of Acts the propagation of His message, the New Testament letters the explanation of His two comings, the Book of Revelation records the consummation of all things in Jesus Christ.

Indeed, we find that everything will be accomplished at the Second Coming of Jesus Christ. We read the following in the Book of Revelation.

Look! He is coming with the clouds; every eye will see him, even those who pierced him; and on his account all the tribes of the earth will wail. So it is to be. Amen (Revelation 1:7 NRSV).

History will reach its climax as Jesus Christ returns to the earth and sets up His everlasting kingdom. Again, this last book of the Bible is all about Jesus.

In sum, we find that Jesus, as He stated, is the main subject of the entire Scripture. Indeed, everything in the Bible is about Him. Consequently, when we read and study Holy Scripture we must always do it from this perspective.

SUMMARY TO QUESTION 2
IS JESUS CHRIST THE MAIN SUBJECT OF THE ENTIRE BIBLE?

Jesus Christ is indeed the theme of the entire Bible. This is the claim He Himself made to the religious leaders of His day. The evidence for this is as follows.

The Old Testament records the preparation for the predicted Deliverer. He is known by a number of names—the most popular being the "Messiah," or "Christ." The kingdom of God would be brought to this earth through the promised Messiah. Everything in the Old Testament looked forward to His arrival.

The four gospels record the fulfillment of the Old Testament predictions concerning the Christ. The things which were predicted of Him were manifested in the Person of Jesus of Nazareth. He had all of the credentials of the coming Messiah. Yet the people rejected Him. Although they put Him to death on the cross of Calvary, death would not hold Him. Three days after His death Jesus the Messiah was alive again.

The Book of Acts continues the biblical pattern—it is all about Jesus. Indeed, it records the proclamation, or propagation of the message of the risen Christ to the known world. Jesus told His disciples to go into the entire world and proclaim the good news, the gospel. Acts records the fulfillment of His command.

The New Testament letters provide the explanation of the two comings of Christ. It tells us Jesus came the first time to die, but He will come again to the earth to rule and reign. Again, it is all about Him.

Finally, the Book of Revelation documents the consummation of all things in Christ. He returns to our world and sets up the promised kingdom. All wrongs will be made right in Jesus Christ.

Therefore, as Jesus claimed so long ago in His discussion with the religious rulers, the entire Bible is truly a great "Him" Book. Indeed, it is all about Him!

QUESTION 3

According To The New Testament, Who Is Jesus?

Whenever we read any book, our goal should always be to discover the intention, or purpose, of the author. As far as the New Testament is concerned, the main character is Jesus Christ and the New Testament was written to create belief in Him. This is the claim it makes for itself. John stated this clearly when he wrote.

> Now Jesus did many other signs in the presence of his disciples, which are not written in this book. But these are written so that you may come to believe that Jesus is the Messiah, the Son of God, and that through believing you may have life in his name (John 20:30,31 NRSV).

These verses are highly instructive. John's purpose in writing was to create in his readers, belief in Jesus as the Christ, the Messiah.

In doing so, he tells us that he was selective in the signs that he recorded about the life and ministry of Jesus, but that the signs that were given were meant to cause the reader to believe. This is John's stated purpose.

The remainder of the New Testament echoes that same purpose. Therefore, we should attempt to discover what Jesus, the main character, actually said and did.

1. THE CLAIM OF THE FOUR GOSPELS: THERE IS ONLY ONE WAY TO REACH THE ONE GOD

When Jesus came to earth, He made a variety of claims about Himself. One thing that Jesus claimed was that He Himself was the only possible way that a person could have a relationship with one true God. There are many people who do not like this assertion because it seems so narrow-minded.

Others try to deny that Jesus said, or meant, this. However, the record is clear. Indeed, whether a person likes it or not, Jesus made the colossal claim that nobody could know the living God except by means of Him. Jesus said the following to the religious leaders of His day.

> That is why I said you will die with your sins unforgiven. If you don't have faith in me for who I am, you will die, and your sins will not be forgiven" (John 8:24 CEV).

Jesus could not be clearer. Unless a person has faith, or believes, in Him, they will not have their sins forgiven.

On the night of His betrayal, Jesus said the following to His disciples who were gathered with Him in the upper room.

> Let not your heart be troubled; you believe in God, believe also in Me (John 14:1 NKJV).

Jesus told people to believe "in Him."

JESUS IS THE ONE WAY TO GOD

In another place, Jesus made it clear that He was the one way to reach the one God. We read the following in John's gospel.

> Jesus said to him, "I am the way, and the truth, and the life. No one comes to the Father except through me" (John 14:6 NRSV).

Notice how exclusive this claim of Jesus is. Nobody can reach God the Father except through Him.

THOSE WHO BELIEVE IN JESUS HAVE ETERNAL LIFE

On another occasion, Christ said that those who believe in Him have passed from death to life. In other words, they already have eternal life.

> Very truly, I tell you, anyone who hears my word and believes him who sent me has eternal life, and does not come under judgment, but has passed from death to life. "Very truly, I tell you, the hour is coming, and is now here, when the dead will hear the voice of the Son of God, and those who hear will live" (John 5:24,25 NRSV).

Anyone who has trusted Jesus as their Savior presently has eternal life. This is His claim.

Elsewhere, Jesus said that those who reject Him will receive God's punishment. We read these difficult words in John's gospel.

> The one who believes in the Son has eternal life, but the one who refuses to believe in the Son will not see life; instead, the wrath of God remains on him (John 3:36 HCSB).

God's wrath will remain upon those who reject Jesus. Therefore, it is crucial that humans put their faith in Him—if they want to have their sins forgiven and have everlasting life.

Again we stress, these are Jesus' claims! He is the One who has said these things about Himself. Consequently, they must be dealt with.

2. THE CLAIMS OF THE BOOK OF ACTS

Not only did the Lord Jesus make exclusive claims about Himself, we also find that the speakers in the Book of Acts also make the claim that Jesus is the only way to reach God.

For example, the Apostle Peter said the following to the religious leaders who had him arrested.

> Salvation is found in no one else, for there is no other name under heaven given to mankind by which we must be saved (Acts 4:12 NIV).

The translation, God's Word, puts it this way.

> No one else can save us. Indeed, we can be saved only by the power of the one named Jesus and not by any other person (Acts 4:12 God's Word).

Note well his claim. There is no salvation outside of the Person of Jesus Christ. He is the only way by which a person can be saved. This echoes what Jesus said about Himself—He is the one way to reach the one God.

3. THE CLAIMS OF PAUL

The writings of the Apostle Paul continue this same line of teaching. He also stated that Jesus Christ was the only way to reach the one, true, God. He wrote the following.

> For there is one God and one intermediary between God and humanity, Christ Jesus, himself human (1 Timothy 2:5 NET).

Paul said that Jesus was the one intermediary, or go-between, between God and the human race. In other words, to reach God, a person must go through Jesus.

When the Apostle Paul wrote to the church at Rome, he taught that it is only through Jesus that a person receives the gift of eternal life. He put it this way.

> For the wages of sin is death, but the free gift of God is eternal life through Christ Jesus our Lord (Romans 6:23 NLT).

Salvation is a free gift from God to those who place their faith in Jesus. We cannot earn it. We can only receive the benefit of what Jesus accomplished on our behalf.

Later, in Romans he wrote of the necessity to believe in Christ. He stated the following.

> Because if you confess with your mouth that Jesus is Lord and believe in your heart that God raised him from the dead, you will be saved. For with the heart one believes and thus has righteousness and with the mouth one confesses and thus has salvation (Romans 10:9,10 NET).

Again, we find the stress is upon believing in Jesus for salvation.

According to Scripture, there is only one God who exists, and only one way to reach Him. It is through Jesus Christ.

4. THE TESTIMONY OF THE BOOK OF HEBREWS

There is still more. The writer to the Hebrews emphasized that Jesus alone saves those who come to God.

> Therefore he is able, once and forever, to save everyone who comes to God through him. He lives forever to plead with God on their behalf (Hebrews 7:25 NLT).

Jesus saves every person who comes to God the Father through Him.

THESE CLAIMS WERE NOT INVENTED BY THE CHURCH

The idea that Jesus is the only way to get to God was not invented by the church. Indeed, it was central to His message. Therefore, according to the New Testament, there is no other way to reach God except through Jesus.

Whether a person believes it or not, the record is clear—Jesus Himself believed and taught that only through Him could a person have their sins forgiven, and come to know the living God. The other New Testament writers proclaimed the same truth.

THERE ARE TWO BASIC QUESTIONS THAT NEED TO BE ANSWERED

Since these are Jesus' claims about Himself there are two basic questions that need to be answered about Him.

QUESTION ONE: WHO DO YOU THINK THAT JESUS IS?

The first question Jesus Himself asked His disciples. We read of this in Matthew.

> He said to them, "But who do you say that I am?" (Matthew 16:15 NKJV).

Who is Jesus Christ to you?

QUESTION TWO: WHAT WILL YOU DO WITH JESUS?

Pontius Pilate asked the second question. Matthew also records this question.

What should I do with Jesus who is called the Messiah? (Matthew 27:22 NLT).

According to Scripture, the eternal destiny of each individual depends upon how we answer these questions. What is your verdict? What have you done with Jesus? Is He your Savior?

SUMMARY TO QUESTION 3
ACCORDING TO THE NEW TESTAMENT, WHO IS JESUS?

The stated purpose of the New Testament is to create belief in the reader that Jesus is the Christ, the Messiah, the Son of God. Those who believe this message receive eternal life. This is why the New Testament was written—to cause people to believe.

As we look at the various writings, which make up the New Testament, we note the consistent theme that Jesus is the one way to reach the one God.

To begin with, Jesus Himself made these claims. Indeed, we find Christ saying that it is through Him alone that a person can receive forgiveness of sin. He also claimed to be the way, the truth, and the life. Nobody could reach God the Father except through Him.

Jesus also said that those who believe in Him presently have everlasting life. There is no doubt that Jesus believed and taught that He alone was the one-way in which a person could reach the one God.

This teaching continued after Jesus' ascension into heaven. In the Book of Acts, we find a number of speeches and sermons recorded. Each speaker made it plain to his audience that salvation was given through Jesus Christ, and Him alone. There is no other way.

The writings of the Apostle Paul teach the same truth. Paul said that Jesus is the one intermediary, or go-between, between God and the human race. To reach God, one must go through Jesus.

We find that writer to the Hebrews also making this claim. Jesus is the One who can save anyone who comes to Him.

These are merely a few of the many references in the New Testament about the importance of Jesus in reaching God the Father. To this we could add much more.

In sum, the specific claim of the New Testament is there is only one God, and only one way to get to the one God, through Jesus Christ. All others are pretenders. Indeed, there is no salvation from sin outside of the Person of Jesus Christ. This is their claim—not something the church later invented.

Therefore, two basic questions about Jesus need to be answered by each individual.

The first is, "Who do you think that He is?" The second question is, "What will you do with Him?"

How we answer these two questions determines how Jesus will judge each and every one of us. Therefore, it is essential that we have the right answers to these questions.

Was Jesus A Human Being?

Throughout the centuries there have been those who questioned the humanity of Jesus. Some have contended that He was not fully human but only "appeared" to be this way. Is this what the New Testament teaches?

To the contrary, the Bible makes it clear that Jesus was indeed fully human. This is seen in the following ways.

Jesus had a human birth, Jesus had a human ancestry, Jesus developed like a normal human being, as the promised Messiah Jesus had to be human, Jesus had the essential elements of a human being—body and spirit, Jesus was given human titles, Jesus was called a man, and finally He showed all the traits of being human.

We can give the following details that support these truths about the nature of Jesus Christ.

1. JESUS HAD A NATURAL HUMAN BIRTH AND CHILDHOOD

To begin with, we find that the circumstances around the birth and childhood of Jesus show that He was fully human. The evidence is as follows.

A. JESUS WAS GIVEN A HUMAN NAME BEFORE HIS BIRTH

Before Jesus was born, the angel of the Lord told Joseph that Mary, to who he was engaged, was going to have a child. Furthermore, Joseph was instructed to name him Jesus. We read the following in Matthew.

> She will bear a son, and you are to name him Jesus, for he will save his people from their sins. All this took place to fulfill what had been spoken by the Lord through the prophet: Look, the virgin shall conceive and bear a son, and they shall name him Emmanuel," which means, "God is with us" (Matthew 1:21-23 NRSV).

Consequently, He was given a human name before birth.

B. JESUS HAD A NORMAL HUMAN BIRTH

Although Jesus was supernaturally conceived, the biblical account of His birth demonstrates that He was a fully human child with a normal human birth. Luke records the circumstances around His birth.

> And she gave birth to her firstborn son and wrapped him in bands of cloth, and laid him in a manger, because there was no place for them in the inn (Luke 2:7 NRSV).

His birth was a natural human birth—like any other child. There was nothing spectacular about it at all.

C. JESUS WAS A HUMAN CHILD

When the shepherds saw the newborn babe, they quickly spread the news to others. Luke records the following.

> And when they saw it, they made known the saying that had been told them concerning this child (Luke 2:17 ESV).

This further emphasizes the fact that He was a genuine child.

When He was eight days old, Jesus was circumcised like other Jewish male children, and brought to the temple for dedication.

> Eight days after his birth, the child was circumcised and named Jesus. This was the name the angel had given him before his mother became pregnant. After the days required by Moses' Teachings to make a mother clean had passed, Joseph and Mary went to Jerusalem. They took Jesus to present him to the Lord (Luke 2:21,22 God's Word).

In this description of His birth, there is no hint that He was anything other than human. While Mary supernaturally conceived a child, His birth was normal. Indeed, the shepherds spread the word about a child that was born.

In the temple, He was dedicated in the same manner as any other male child. Although His conception was supernatural, His birth was that of a normal, fully human child. The Apostle Paul wrote.

> But when the fullness of time had come, God sent his Son, born of a woman, born under the law (Galatians 4:4 NRSV).

This is another testimony to His humanity.

2. JESUS HAD A HUMAN ANCESTRY

In addition, we find that the genealogy of Jesus Christ links Him to the rest of humanity. In Luke's Gospel, His family line is traced all the way back to Adam, the first human. We read.

> Kenan was the son of Enosh. Enosh was the son of Seth. Seth was the son of Adam. Adam was the son of God (Luke 3:38 NLT).

His family line consists of human beings. They are actual historical characters. In fact, Bible speaks about many of them.

Therefore, everything that Scripture has to say about His birth indicates that Jesus was a genuine human child. The remainder of Jesus' life testifies to the fact of His humanity.

A. HE DEVELOPED LIKE A NORMAL HUMAN BEING

The Scripture states that the child Jesus grew in both size and wisdom. Luke records what occurred as follows.

> So Jesus grew both in height and in wisdom, and he was loved by God and by all who knew him (Luke 2:52 NLT).

Growing in size, and intellectual ability, is a human trait. Therefore, this summary statement of His early years testifies to His humanity.

After this, the boy grew to be a man. This is further testimony to His humanity.

B. JESUS WAS PART OF A FAMILY

The New Testament says that Jesus had a family. His mother was named Mary and He had four brothers and at least two sisters. In Matthew, we read about those in Nazareth testifying to His family members.

> Isn't this the carpenter? Isn't this Mary's son and the brother of James, Joseph, Judas and Simon? Aren't his sisters here with us?" And they took offense at him (Mark 6:3 NIV).

All of this points to Jesus being fully human.

3. AS THE MESSIAH HE WOULD BE HUMAN

There is something else. The promised Messiah of the Old Testament was to be a human being. The evidence for this can be seen as follows.

A. HE WAS A PHYSICAL DESCENDANT OF KING DAVID

Jesus was the promised Messiah. The Messiah was to be a physical descendant of King David—a human being. We read that God promised David the following.

When your days are fulfilled and you lie down with your fathers, I will raise up your offspring after you, . . . your house and your kingdom shall be made sure forever before me. Your throne shall be established forever (2 Samuel 7:12,16 ESV).

The promised Messiah, who would rule forever, would be a descendant of David. This clearly shows that the Messiah would be human.

Paul wrote about the human Jesus being David's descendant. He put it this way in his letter to the Romans.

From Paul, a servant of Jesus Christ, called to be an apostle and appointed to spread the Good News of God. (God had already promised this Good News through his prophets in the Holy Scriptures. This Good News is about his Son, our Lord Jesus Christ. In his human nature he was a descendant of David. In his spiritual, holy nature he was declared the Son of God. This was shown in a powerful way when he came back to life (Romans 1:1-4 God's Word).

The fact that Jesus was born as a descendant of King David further testifies to His humanity.

B. THE MESSIAH WAS TO BE THE OFFSPRING OF THE WOMAN

He was the predicted "offspring (seed) of the woman." This also indicates true humanity. We read the following in the Book of Genesis.

And I will put enmity between you and the woman, and between your offspring and hers; he will crush your head, and you will strike his heel (Genesis 3:15 NIV).

Jesus was physically related to the first woman—Eve.

C. THE MESSIAH IS A PROPHET LIKE MOSES

We also find that the Messiah was to be a prophet like Moses, a human being. Moses said to the people.

The LORD your God will raise up for you a prophet like me from among your own brothers. You must listen to him (Deuteronomy 18:15 NRSV).

Moses said the Messiah would be like him in the sense that He would be from the nation Israel. The Scriptures are clear that the Messiah was to be a human being.

D. HE WAS FROM THE NATION ISRAEL

The New Testament says that Jesus, the Messiah, was recognized as being from the nation Israel. Paul wrote to the Romans.

They are the descendants of Israel, and they are also God's chosen people. God showed them his glory. He made agreements with them and gave them his Law. The temple is theirs and so are the promises that God made to them. They have those famous ancestors, who were also the ancestors of Jesus Christ (Romans 9:4,5 CEV).

This is another indication of Jesus' genuine humanity. He was from the "chosen people."

We read in John's gospel how a Samaritan woman identified Jesus as a Jew. The Bible explains it this way.

"How is it that You, a Jew, ask for a drink from me, a Samaritan woman?" she asked Him. For Jews do not associate with Samaritans (John 4:9 HCSB).

The fact that Jesus was Jewish was obvious.

Later we read in John's gospel about how Jesus outwardly appeared to people. We find that He was a man less than fifty years of age. The Bible says.

Then the Jews said to Him, "You are not yet fifty years old, and have You seen Abraham?" (John 8:57 NKJV).

Jesus looked like a grown man who had not yet reached the age of fifty. This is another indication of His humanity.

4. JESUS HAD THE ESSENTIALS ELEMENTS OF A HUMAN BEING—A BODY AND A SPIRIT

The Bible says that Jesus possessed the essential elements of human nature—a human body, and a human spirit. It is obvious that He had a body in that He could touch people. We read about this in Matthew.

> He [Jesus] stretched out his hand and touched him, saying, "I do choose. Be made clean!" Immediately his leprosy was cleansed (Matthew 8:3 NRSV).

To be able to physically touch another person Jesus had to be human.

We also find that His body could bleed. On the cross, He bled when a Roman soldier thrust a spear into His side. John wrote.

> One of the soldiers, however, pierced his side with a spear, and blood and water flowed out (John 19:34 NLT).

Again, this is another sign of His true humanity. Only genuine humans can bleed.

Jesus Christ also had a spirit. Mark wrote.

> At once Jesus perceived in his spirit that they were discussing these questions among themselves; and he said to them, "Why do you raise such questions in your hearts?" (Mark 2:8 NRSV).

Having a human spirit is another indication of His genuine humanity.

5. JESUS WAS GIVEN HUMAN TITLES

Human titles were ascribed to Jesus. They include the following.

A. JESUS WAS THE LAST ADAM, THE SECOND MAN

Jesus was called the "last Adam" and the "second man." Paul the apostle wrote.

> Thus it is written, "The first man, Adam, became a living being"; the last Adam became a life-giving spirit. But it is not the spiritual that is first, but the physical, and then the spiritual. The first man was from the earth, a man of dust; the second man is from heaven" (1 Corinthians 15:45-47 NRSV).

Adam was the first human who was created perfect. Jesus was the last human being who was perfect humanity. Adam did not remain perfect, while Jesus did.

B. JESUS IS THE INTERMEDIARY BETWEEN GOD AND HUMANITY

Jesus was called an intermediary, or go-between, between God and humanity. Paul wrote about this to Timothy.

> For there is one God and one intermediary between God and humanity, Christ Jesus, himself human (1 Timothy 2:5 NET).

To be an intermediary Christ had to be human.

6. HE WAS CALLED A MAN

The New Testament records Jesus calling Himself a man. Furthermore, others called Him a man.

A. JESUS CALLED HIMSELF A MAN

Jesus expressly called Himself a man! He said to the religious leaders.

> But now you are trying to kill me, a man who has told you the truth that I heard from God. This is not what Abraham did (John 8:40 NRSV).

Jesus never gave the impression that He was non-human in any way.

The New Testament writers recognized the humanity of Jesus. The apostles Peter, Paul, and John all emphasized the humanity of Jesus in their writings.

B. PETER SAID HE JESUS WAS A MAN

On the Day of Pentecost, Peter said the following about Jesus to a large crowd that had gathered.

> Men of Israel, listen to these words: This Jesus the Nazarene was a man pointed out to you by God with miracles, wonders, and signs that God did among you through Him, just as you yourselves know (Acts 2:22 HCSB).

According to Peter, Jesus was a genuine man—a man from Nazareth.

C. PAUL TAUGHT THAT JESUS WAS HUMAN

The Apostle Paul wrote about Jesus' humanity. In the introduction to his letter to the Romans, we read the following.

> This good news is about his Son, our Lord Jesus Christ! As a human, he was from the family of David. But the Holy Spirit proved that Jesus is the powerful Son of God, because he was raised from death. (Romans 1:3-4 CEV).

Jesus came from the human line of David.

Later in his letter, Paul again wrote to the Romans how Christ was a human being.

> What the law could not do since it was limited by the flesh, God did. He condemned sin in the flesh by sending His own Son in flesh like ours under sin's domain, and as a sin offering (Romans 8:3 HCSB).

God sent His "own Son" in the flesh. In other words, He became a human being.

Paul wrote to Timothy about the mystery, or sacred secret, that had now been revealed—Christ appeared in a body.

> Beyond all question, the mystery of godliness is great: He appeared in a body, was vindicated by the Spirit, was seen by angels, was preached among the nations, was believed on in the world, was taken up in glory (1 Timothy 3:16 NIV).

The great mystery is that God the Son became a human being.

D. JOHN TAUGHT THAT JESUS WAS HUMAN

In fact, John said that it was the false prophets that denied that Jesus came in the flesh—that He was a human being. We read the following in First John.

> Dear friends, don't believe all people who say that they have the Spirit. Instead, test them. See whether the spirit they have is from God, because there are many false prophets in the world. This is how you can recognize God's Spirit: Every person who declares that Jesus Christ has come as a human has the Spirit that is from God. But every person who doesn't declare that Jesus Christ has come as a human has a spirit that isn't from God. This is the spirit of the antichrist that you have heard is coming. That spirit is already in the world (1 John 4:1-3 God's Word).

Interestingly, they denied Jesus' humanity, not His deity. They could believe that He was God, but not that He was genuinely human.

Elsewhere, John wrote about those deceivers. We read.

> Many deceivers have gone out into the world, those who do not confess that Jesus Christ has come in the flesh; any such person is the deceiver and the antichrist! (2 John 7 NRSV).

They rejected the fact that Jesus was actually human.

E. HE WAS AN UNCOMMON MAN

Those who came into contact with Jesus realized that He was an uncommon man, but they also understood that He was a real or genuine man. When the religious leaders sent their officers to apprehend Jesus they came back empty handed. They explained it as follows.

> When the temple police returned to the chief priests and Pharisees, they were asked, "Why didn't you bring Jesus here?" They answered, "No one has ever spoken like that man!" (John 7:25-46 CEV).

Jesus spoke as no man has spoken—either before or since.

His disciples certainly recognized His uniqueness. When Jesus calmed the storm on the Sea of Galilee we read of their response.

> They were overcome with fear and asked each other, "Who is this man? Even the wind and the sea obey him" (Mark 4:41 God's Word).

Even though He had authority over nature, Jesus was still regarded as a man.

7. JESUS SHOWED ALL THE TRAITS OF A HUMAN BEING

Jesus demonstrated that He had all the traits of a human. We can give the following examples.

A. JESUS WAS TEMPTED

Jesus was tempted by the devil. Matthew records it as follows.

> Then the Spirit led Jesus into the desert to be tempted by the devil (Matthew 4:1 God's Word).

Only human beings can be tempted.

B. HE EXPERIENCED HUNGER

After His baptism in the Jordan River, Jesus was led by the Spirit out into the wilderness. The Bible says that He became hungry.

> After He had fasted 40 days and 40 nights, He was hungry (Matthew 4:2 HCSB).

Here Jesus exhibits the human trait of hunger. Like other human beings, a long period without food made Him hungry.

C. JESUS EXPERIENCED THIRST

Jesus also experienced thirst while suffering on the cross. John records what occurred.

> After this, when Jesus knew that all was now finished, he said (in order to fulfill the scripture), "I am thirsty" (John 19:28 NRSV).

This is another indication of Jesus' humanity.

D. JESUS ATE AND DRANK WITH OTHERS

Jesus ate and drank with others—mingling among humanity as a fellow human being. We read the following in the Gospel of Matthew.

> John the Baptist did not go around eating and drinking, and you said, "That man has a demon in him!" But the Son of Man goes around eating and drinking, and you say, "That man eats and drinks too much! He is even a friend of tax collectors and sinners." Yet Wisdom is shown to be right by what it does (Matthew 11:18,19 CEV).

He was able to participate in eating and drinking.

E. JESUS BECAME TIRED

Early in His ministry, the Bible speaks of Jesus being tired from a long trip. John records the following took place.

Jacob's well was there, and Jesus, tired out by his journey, was sitting by the well. It was about noon (John 4:6 NRSV).

The fact that He could become tired shows He was a genuine human.

F. JESUS HAD TO SLEEP

We are also told that Jesus needed sleep. Matthew wrote about Jesus falling asleep while on a boat sailing on the Sea of Galilee.

Suddenly, a terrible storm came up, with waves breaking into the boat. But Jesus was sleeping (Matthew 8:24 NLT).

He had no special ability to stay awake all the time.

G. JESUS ASKED QUESTIONS

Another indication of the humanity of Jesus is that He asked questions. Sometimes Jesus asked questions that were rhetorical. In other words, He was not expecting an answer.

Other questions were intended to make His followers think.

At times, Jesus asked questions because He wanted information. We read in Mark.

"How long has this been happening?" Jesus asked the boy's father. He replied, "Since he was very small" (Mark 9:21 NLT).

Therefore, there were some questions that were asked with a genuine desire to gather information. In another example, in the city of Bethany, Jesus asked the location of the tomb of Lazarus.

And He said, "Where have you laid him?" They said to Him, "Lord, come and see" (John 11:34 NKJV).

These questions show that His human nature was real.

H. JESUS SHOWED HUMAN EMOTIONS

Jesus also expressed human emotions such as tears, love, compassion, disappointment, and anger. For example, at the tomb of His dead friend Lazarus, Scripture records, "Jesus burst into tears" (John 11:35). He also cried over the city of Jerusalem. Luke records.

> As he approached Jerusalem and saw the city, he wept over it (Luke 19:41 NIV).

He had human feelings that allowed Him to cry at a tragic situation.

JESUS COULD GIVE AND RECEIVE LOVE

Like other human beings, Jesus could give and receive love. We are told that Jesus loved a certain ruler.

> Jesus felt genuine love for this man as he looked at him. "You lack only one thing," he told him. "Go and sell all you have and give the money to the poor, and you will have treasure in heaven. Then come, follow me:" (Mark 10:21 NLT).

The trait of love is another indication of His humanity.

JESUS EXPRESSED COMPASSION

Jesus could feel compassion for others. Matthew writes.

> When He saw the crowds, He felt compassion for them, because they were weary and worn out, like sheep without a shepherd (Matthew 9:36 HCSB).

The fact that Jesus could be moved with compassion when looking at the multitudes is further evidence of His true humanity.

JESUS COULD BE DISAPPOINTED

Jesus could also experience disappointment. We read the following episode in Mark.

Now the next day, when they had come out from Bethany, He was hungry. And seeing from afar a fig tree having leaves, He went to see if perhaps He would find something on it. When He came to it, He found nothing but leaves, for it was not the season for figs (Mark 11:12,13 NKJV).

This incident further illustrates His humanity.

JESUS BECAME ANGRY

We also find that Jesus was angry for the way the religious rulers were corrupting the temple practices. John records His anger.

When He had made a whip of cords, He drove them all out of the temple, with the sheep and the oxen, and poured out the changers' money and overturned the tables. And He said to those who sold doves, "Take these things away! Do not make My Father's house a house of merchandise!" (John 2:15,16 NKJV).

Anger is appropriate in certain situations. Jesus, in His humanity, showed godly anger.

JESUS COULD BECOME UPSET

The Bible says that Jesus was upset at the prospect of having the penalty for the sins of the world placed upon Him. John records Jesus saying the following.

Now I am deeply troubled, and I don't know what to say. But I must not ask my Father to keep me from this time of suffering. In fact, I came into the world to suffer. So Father, bring glory to yourself (John 12:27,28 CEV).

He could feel troubled.

Jesus was troubled by the betrayal of Judas Iscariot. We read in John's gospel.

After saying this Jesus was troubled in spirit, and declared, "Very truly, I tell you, one of you will betray me" (John 13:21 NRSV).

These various human emotions are further indications that His humanity was genuine.

I. JESUS, LIKE OTHER HUMANS, PRAYED

Only humans can pray to God. Jesus prayed often. The writer to the Hebrews noted this.

> While Jesus was here on earth, he offered prayers and pleadings, with a loud cry and tears, to the one who could deliver him out of death. And God heard his prayers because of his reverence for God (Hebrews 5:7 NLT).

The fact that Jesus felt the need to pray shows He was indeed human.

J. JESUS SUFFERED PAIN

Jesus suffered pain like other humans. Luke writes about His suffering in the Garden of Gethsemane.

> He prayed more fervently, and he was in such agony of spirit that his sweat fell to the ground like great drops of blood (Luke 22:44 NLT).

As a human, Jesus suffered.

The Romans flogged Him.

> Then Pilate had Jesus flogged with a lead-tipped whip (John 19:1 NLT).

This would have caused much physical pain. There is no evidence whatsoever, that God intervened so that Jesus would not experience the pain.

K. JESUS EXPERIENCED DEATH

Like other humans, He died. John writes.

> When they came to Jesus, they did not break His legs since they saw that He was already dead. When they came to Jesus, they did not break His legs since they saw that He was already dead (John 19:33 HSCB).

If Jesus Christ were not a real human being, then His death on Calvary's cross was merely an illusion. But Scripture emphasizes that it was not illusory. He truly died.

THE UNITED TESTIMONY OF SCRIPTURE: JESUS WAS HUMAN

In sum, the Scriptures are united in their testimony to the genuine humanity of Jesus. There is never any indication given that He was somehow non-human. He experienced growth, hunger, tiredness, sadness and death—just as other human beings experience. He was not given any special immunity from these experiences.

This is important for us to realize. He was born, He lived, and He died— experiencing the same things we do. Therefore, He is able to identify with our feelings when we pray to the Father through Him. The writer to Hebrews said.

> Because he himself was tested by what he suffered, he is able to help those who are being tested (Hebrews 2:18 NRSV).

There was no special treatment given Jesus while He was here upon earth. He felt the same things as every other human being feels.

The fact that Jesus' humanity was genuine is made clear by the united testimony of Scripture. Indeed, the reality of the humanity of Jesus Christ is at the center of any true conception of who He is.

SUMMARY TO QUESTION 4
WAS JESUS A HUMAN BEING?

When we explore the subject of the humanity of Jesus Christ, the Scripture is clear, Jesus was indeed human. He had all the traits that make up a human being—except that He was without sin.

Like all other humans He was born into the world through a human birth. As was the custom with Jewish male children, He was circumcised on the eighth day. Everything having to do with His birth indicates Jesus' genuine humanity.

His genealogy consists entirely of human beings. In fact, Jesus is linked to Adam, the first human.

In addition, the Old Testament predicted that the coming Messiah would be human, a man like Moses. He would also be a physical descendant of King David. Jesus, as the Messiah, had to have been human.

From the four gospels we find that He had a family with four brothers, and at least two sisters. This is another indication of His human nature.

The Bible says that Jesus was a human child who grew to be a man. We find that He possessed the essential elements of humanity—a body and a spirit. As a man, He was hungry, tired, and needed sleep. Jesus Himself, as well as others, admitted that He was human.

Furthermore, Jesus showed human emotions such as love, tears, hate, disappointment and compassion. In all of this, there is not the slightest indication that Jesus was anything other than human.

Only humans can pray to God, and we find Jesus praying to God. This is further evidence of His true humanity.

Finally, we find that Jesus experienced pain, and death. This, of course, is something that humanity universally experiences.

Therefore, it is the united testimony of the New Testament that Jesus Christ was fully human. There is certainly no doubt about this.

Does The New Testament Give Direct Evidence That Jesus Is God?

The Scripture teaches that Jesus Christ was truly human. There is no doubt about this. In modern times, however, there remains the question concerning His deity. Was He more than just a man?

JESUS WAS FULLY HUMAN AND FULLY GOD

The Scriptures testify that Jesus was fully human and also fully God. This can be observed from Jesus' own testimony, and the testimony of others. We find this to be true in both direct and indirect statements about Him.

There are a number of direct statements in the New Testament concerning the deity of Christ. They include the following.

1. THE TESTIMONY OF THE FOUR GOSPELS

The four gospels testify to Jesus' deity. We will list some of the evidence that they provide.

A. JESUS WAS IN THE BEGINNING WITH GOD

The Bible says that Jesus Christ has always existed. John starts his gospel as follows.

> In the beginning was the Word, and the Word was with God, and the Word was God (John 1:1 KJV).

This statement is clear. Jesus Christ was in the beginning with God—because He is God. The imperfect tense of the verb stresses the fact that Jesus continually existed in the past. As far back as one goes in time, Jesus Christ is already there.

B. JESUS IS "HIMSELF GOD"

John also made this claim about Jesus.

> No one has ever seen God. The only one, himself God, who is in closest fellowship with the Father, has made God known (John 1:18 NET)

Here Jesus is called God. Jesus, therefore, is unique in His relationship with God the Father.

C. JESUS IS EQUAL WITH GOD

Jesus Christ also claimed equality with God. The following account in John's gospel reveals this about Him.

> This is why the Jews began trying all the more to kill Him: not only was He breaking the Sabbath, but He was even calling God His own Father, making Himself equal with God (John 5:18 HCSB).

The Jews wanted to kill Jesus because they understood that He was claiming equality with God. As His contemporaries, they certainly knew what He was saying about Himself. Indeed, because of His claim they wanted to put Him to death.

D. JESUS EXISTED BEFORE ABRAHAM

Although Jesus was born as a babe in Bethlehem, He claimed to have existed two thousand years earlier at the time of Abraham. John records the following.

Jesus said to them, "I tell you the solemn truth, before Abraham came into existence, I am!" (John 8:58 NET).

While angels, and other created heavenly beings, existed before Abraham, Jesus never claimed to be a mere angel or some other type of created being.

E. THOMAS' CONFESSION OF JESUS

Jesus made Himself equal with God. When doubting Thomas saw the risen Christ, he gave testimony to Jesus' deity.

Thomas answered him, "My Lord and my God!" (John 20:28 NRSV).

Thomas confessed to Jesus' deity. Jesus did not rebuke Him for this. To the contrary, we find that the Lord had the following response.

Jesus said to him, "Have you believed because you have seen me? Blessed are the people who have not seen and yet have believed" (John 20:29 NET).

Jesus acknowledged the confession of Thomas. Jesus is indeed Lord and God!

2. THE TESTIMONY OF THE BOOK OF ACTS

In the Book of Acts, written by Luke, we seem to have a direct statement about Christ's deity. He wrote of the apostle Paul speaking of the "church of God" that was purchased "with His own blood."

Be on guard for yourselves and for all the flock, among whom the Holy Spirit has appointed you as overseers, to shepherd the church of God, which He purchased with His own blood. (Acts 20:28 HCSB).

It was the blood of Jesus Christ that paid the penalty for our sin. Yet, here it says that "God" bought the church with His own blood. Consequently, it is saying that Jesus Christ is God.

We should note, however, that the reading "His own blood" is uncertain—there is a variation in the manuscripts at this point. Some manuscripts read, "the blood of His own Son" instead of "His own blood." For example, the New Revised Standard Version says.

> Keep watch over yourselves and over all the flock, of which the Holy Spirit has made you overseers, to shepherd the church of God that he obtained with the blood of his own Son (Acts 20:28 NRSV).

Therefore, it is uncertain as to whether this is a reference to the deity of Christ.

3. THE WRITINGS OF PAUL

The Apostle Paul made a number of statements about Jesus deity. He believed that Jesus was indeed God Himself. They include the following statements.

A. JESUS IS GOD OVER ALL

Paul said that Jesus was God over all. He wrote to the Romans.

> Their ancestors were great people of God, and Christ himself was a Jew as far as his human nature is concerned. And he is God, who rules over everything and is worthy of eternal praise! Amen (Romans 9:5 NLT).

Christ is God. Indeed, He is the One who rules over everything.

B. JESUS IS YAHWEH (LORD)

Paul wrote to the Romans that Jesus is Lord, or *Yahweh*. We read the following.

If you confess with your mouth, "Jesus is Lord," and believe in your heart that God raised Him from the dead, you will be saved. With the heart one believes, resulting in righteousness, and with the mouth one confesses, resulting in salvation (Romans 10:9,10 HCSB).

To be saved, a person needs to confess Jesus as the Lord—that He is Yahweh, the divine name for God.

C. JESUS HAS THE SAME NATURE AS GOD

Jesus Christ has the same nature as the one, true God. Paul wrote about this in his letter to the Philippians. He put it this way.

Your attitude should be the same that Christ Jesus had. Though he was God, he did not demand and cling to his rights as God (Philippians 2:5,6 NLT).

Jesus is the one, true God who humbly came to our planet. In doing so, He did not demand all of His rights as God.

D. HE IS THE VISIBLE IMAGE OF THE INVISIBLE GOD

When Paul wrote to the Colossians He said a number of important things about Jesus' identity. First, He said that Jesus Christ is the image of the invisible God. In addition, He is pre-eminent over all creation.

Furthermore, he said that Jesus existed before "all things." These statements stress His eternal existence. Paul wrote.

The Son is the image of the invisible God, the firstborn over all creation. For in him all things were created: things in heaven and on earth, visible and invisible, whether thrones or powers or rulers or authorities; all things have been created through him and for him. He is before all things, and in him all things hold together (Colossians 1:15-17 NIV).

The translation, God's Word, puts it this way.

> Christ is exactly like God, who cannot be seen. He is the first- born Son, superior to all creation. Everything was created by him, everything in heaven and on earth, everything seen and unseen, including all forces and powers, and all rulers and authorities. All things were created by God's Son, and everything was made for him. God's Son was before all else, and by him everything is held together (Colossians 1:15-17 God's Word).

Jesus Christ is fully God. There is no doubt about this.

E. JESUS HAS ALL THE FULLNESS OF DEITY

Later in Colossians, Paul said that all the fullness of deity is in Jesus. Indeed, he specifically said the following.

> For in Christ the fullness of God lives in a human body (Colossians 2:9 NLT).

It could not be clearer than this—Jesus was fully God and fully human.

F. JESUS IS THE GREAT GOD AND SAVIOR

Jesus is also called the great God and Savior. Paul wrote about this to Titus.

> At the same time we can expect what we hope for—the appearance of the glory of our great God and Savior, Jesus Christ (Titus 2:13 God's Word).

Jesus Christ is our great God and Savior. The verse is not speaking of the appearing of two distinct persons, the great God, and the Savior. Rather it speaks of the appearing of one Person—Jesus, who is the great God and Savior!

IT IS BEYOND ALL DOUBT IN ORIGINAL GREEK

This is clear beyond any doubt in the original Greek. There is a rule in Greek grammar known as the Granville-Sharp rule. It can be very simply stated as follows: when two nouns in the singular are joined by the word "and" (*kai* in Greek) and the first noun has the article in front of it, and the second noun does not, both nouns refer to the same thing.

In Titus 2:13 we have this type of construction. The first noun "God" has the Greek article in front of it. The second noun "Savior" does not. They are joined together by the Greek word *kai* translated as "and." Therefore, the great God and Savior are the same person, Jesus Christ. There is no getting around this grammatical rule.

Please note that this is a simplified explanation of the rule. The rule is a bit more complicated than we have stated it. Nevertheless, the conclusion remains that Titus 2:13 is a direct statement of Jesus' deity.

4. THE TESTIMONY OF THE BOOK OF HEBREWS

The writer to the Hebrews accepted the deity of Jesus Christ. The Son is directly called God. The Father says that throne of the Son will last forever and ever. We read.

> But to the Son He says "Your throne, O God, is forever and ever; A scepter of righteousness is the scepter of Your Kingdom" (Hebrews 1:8 NKJV).

The Son is directly called God by God the Father. The Father, of course, would certainly be in a position to know this!

5. PETER

Peter, one of Jesus' own disciples, confessed to His deity. Jesus Christ is called both God and Savior by Peter.

> Simeon Peter, a slave and an apostle of Jesus Christ: To those who have obtained a faith of equal privilege with

ours through the righteousness of our God and Savior Jesus Christ (2 Peter 1:1 HCSB).

This Greek construction is another example of the Granville-Sharp rule. God and Savior speak of the same Person, Jesus.

6. JOHN

From the First letter of John, we have another statement about the deity of Christ. John wrote that Jesus is the one, true God. He explained it in this manner.

> And we know that the Son of God has come and has given us insight to know him who is true, and we are in him who is true, in his Son Jesus Christ. This one is the true God and eternal life (1 John 5:20 NET).

The translation God's Word renders the verse in this manner.

> We know that the Son of God has come and has given us understanding so that we know the real God. We are in the one who is real, his Son Jesus Christ. This Jesus Christ is the real God and eternal life (1 John 5:20 God's Word).

Hence, John gives a clear statement to the deity of Christ.

In sum, as we examine the totality of the New Testament we find direct evidence that Jesus Christ is called "God." Of this, there is no doubt.

SUMMARY TO QUESTION 5
DOES THE NEW TESTAMENT GIVE DIRECT EVIDENCE THAT JESUS IS GOD?

As we survey the New Testament, we find direct statements about the deity of Jesus Christ from five different New Testament writers. John, Luke, Paul, the writer to the Hebrews, and Peter. They all testified directly that Jesus Christ was more than a mere human being—He is God Almighty.

It is claimed that He was in the beginning with God. In other words, when all things began, Jesus had already existed. Indeed, Scripture says He is the Creator of all things.

Furthermore, He is called "Himself God" in the Gospel of John. This is a further reference to His deity. In fact, John emphasizes the special relationship Jesus had with God the Father.

Jesus also claimed equality with God. John records the Jewish religious leaders attempted to stone Him to death because of these claims.

The Apostle Thomas worshipped Him as God when Jesus appeared alive eight days after His death. Jesus accepted Thomas' confession that He was both Lord and God.

While the Bible says that Jesus' blood paid the penalty for sin, it also says that the blood of God bought the church. Thus, it logically follows that Jesus is God.

Paul said that all of the fullness of God resided in Jesus. This further indicates Jesus' deity. Indeed, this could be said of nobody else.

Both Peter and Paul say that Jesus is the great God and Savior. Indeed, their statements are about as clear as can be.

In his first letter to believers, John the Apostle wrote that Jesus is the one, true God.

In the Book of Hebrews, God the Father is recorded as calling the Son "God." This is another text which indicates Jesus was more than a mere human.

It is plain from the above references that the writers of the New Testament believed that Jesus is God Himself.

Does The Bible Indirectly Teach That Jesus Is God?

The New Testament gives direct evidence that Jesus is God. Indeed, a number of passages make this beyond all doubt. However, there is more—Scripture also provides indirect evidence for the deity of Jesus Christ.

There are many indirect references that could be cited. They include the following testimony.

JESUS POSSESSES THE ATTRIBUTES OF DEITY

According to Scripture, Jesus possessed certain attributes that belong to God alone.

1. JESUS IS ALL-KNOWING

Jesus is said to have been all-knowing. Christ knew the thoughts of people. Luke writes about this in his gospel. He put it this way.

> Jesus knew what they were thinking. So he told the man to stand up where everyone could see him. And the man stood up (Luke 6:8 CEV).

While some believe this is Jesus merely perceiving what people were thinking by their expressions, it seems to mean much more than this.

We find that Jesus was able to tell the Samaritan woman her past history without having previously met her. Jesus said.

> For you have had five husbands, and the one whom you now have is not your husband; in that you spoke truly (John 4:18 NKJV).

Jesus knew all of these things about her—without having ever met the woman.

This Samaritan woman later testified to His supernatural knowledge when she said the following to the people of her village.

> Come and see a man who told me everything I have ever done! He cannot be the Messiah, can he? (John 4:29 NRSV).

He knew things that mere humans do not have the ability to know.

The disciples of Jesus recognized this fact. They said the following words to Him on the night of His betrayal.

> Now we know that you know all things, and do not need to have anyone question you; by this we believe that you came from God (John 16:30 NRSV).

This unique ability of Jesus was recognized by His disciples.

We also read elsewhere in John's gospel of the complete knowledge of Jesus. He records the following exchange between Jesus and Simon Peter.

> Jesus asked him a third time, "Simon, son of John, do you love me?" Peter felt sad because Jesus had asked him a third time, "Do you love me?" So Peter said to him, "Lord, you know everything. You know that I love you." Jesus told him, "Feed my sheep" (John 21:17 God's Word).

Peter recognized Jesus' ability to know all things.

In the Book of Acts, we read of Jesus' disciples acknowledging His ability to know the hearts of everyone.

> And they prayed and said, "You, O Lord, who know the hearts of all, show which of these two You have chosen" (Acts 1:24 NKJV).

They realized the extent of His knowledge—it was unlimited.

Jesus demonstrated knowledge about things that only someone who is all-knowing could know. This includes things which will take place in the future. We read the following predictions of Jesus in Matthew.

> From then on Jesus began to point out to His disciples that He must go to Jerusalem and suffer many things from the elders, chief priests, and scribes, be killed, and be raised the third day (Matthew 16:21 HCSB).

These predictions came true—just as Jesus said. The evidence from Scripture is that Jesus is all-knowing. Of course, being all-knowing, or omniscient, is something which belongs to God alone.

2. JESUS IS EVERYWHERE PRESENT

Jesus said that He is present with believers everywhere. Matthew records Him making the following statement.

> For where two or three are gathered together in My name, I am there in the midst of them (Matthew 18:20 NKJV).

Wherever believers gather, Jesus is there.

At the end of Matthew's Gospel, Jesus said that He would always be with His disciples.

Teach these new disciples to obey all the commands I have given you. And be sure of this: I am with you always, even to the end of the age (Matthew 28:20 NLT).

This is a wonderful promise of Jesus. He will be with those who are His until the end of this present age.

The Apostle Paul wrote to the Ephesians about the fact that Jesus is everywhere-present. He explained it in this manner.

And the church is his body; it is filled by Christ, who fills everything everywhere with his presence (Ephesians 1:23 NLT).

Jesus' presence is everywhere.

Paul also wrote to the Ephesians about the presence of Jesus Christ extending to the entire universe. He said.

He who descended is the very one who ascended higher than all the heavens, in order to fill the whole universe (Ephesians 4:10 NIV).

The fact that Jesus is everywhere present is taught in Scripture. This is another indication of His deity—since only God can be everywhere present.

3. JESUS' NATURE IS UNCHANGEABLE

The character of Jesus does not change. Indeed, the writer to the Hebrews said He remains the same forever.

Jesus Christ the same yesterday, and today, and forever (Hebrews 13:8 KJV).

Only God is unchangeable in His nature. This is another indication that Jesus Christ is the eternal God.

4. JESUS HAS LIFE IN HIMSELF

The Bible says that Jesus has life in Himself. John wrote.

> In him was life; and the life was the light of men (John 1:4
> KJV).

Later, in John's gospel, we read of Jesus claiming to be "the life."

> Jesus said to him, "I am the way, and the truth, and the life.
> No one comes to the Father except through me" (John 14:6
> NRSV).

All other creation, humans, animals, and plants, are alive because someone, or something else, has given it to them. Jesus has life in Himself—it is not derived from any other source. This is a further indication of His deity.

5. JESUS IS ALL-POWERFUL

Jesus is also said to be all-powerful, or omnipotent. This is an attribute which belongs to God alone. Jesus Himself claimed this. We read.

> Jesus came to them and said: I have been given all authority
> in heaven and on earth! (Matthew 28:18 CEV).

The fact that Jesus is all knowing, everywhere present, unchangeable, has life in Himself, and is all-powerful, demonstrates that He is God. Indeed, these attributes belong to God alone. Nobody, human, angel, or any other created being, could claim them.

6. JESUS HAS EXISTED FOR ALL ETERNITY

There is more evidence. The Scripture teaches the eternality of Jesus. This means that Jesus Christ has existed for all eternity. There was never a time when He did not exist. The biblical testimony is as follows.

A. THE TESTIMONY OF JOHN

The Apostle John wrote that Jesus existed prior to the creation of the universe. In the very first verse of his gospel, he said the following.

> In the beginning was the Word, and the Word was with God and the Word was God (John 1:1 KJV).

As far back as we go, Jesus is already there.

Jesus Himself prayed that God the Father would restore His eternal glory to Him. On the night of His betrayal, Jesus said.

> So now, Father, glorify me in your own presence with the glory that I had in your presence before the world existed (John 17:5 NRSV).

Jesus was in the Father's presence, with all of His glory, before the world had been created. This is certainly a sign of deity.

We are told that Isaiah the prophet also saw Jesus' glory and actually spoke of Him. John wrote about this in his gospel.

> These things Isaiah said when he saw His glory and spoke of Him (John 12:41 NKJV).

The reference to Isaiah seeing the glory of Jesus is found in Isaiah 6:1-3. It reads as follows.

> In the year that King Uzziah died, I saw the Lord seated on a throne, high and exalted, and the train of his robe filled the temple. Above him were seraphs, each with six wings: With two wings they covered their faces, with two they covered their feet, and with two they were flying. And they were calling to one another: "Holy, holy, holy is the LORD Almighty; the whole earth is full of his glory" (Isaiah 6:1-3 NIV).

The fact that Jesus has existed for all eternity is also known as the "doctrine of eternality." It is sometimes equated with the doctrine of pre-existence.

However, the pre-existence of Christ merely means that He existed before He was born. It does not necessarily mean that He existed eternally—but it could mean that.

B. THE TESTIMONY OF JOHN THE BAPTIST

Although John the Baptist was born before Jesus, John testified that Jesus existed before him. It says in the gospel of John.

> John testified to him and cried out, "This was he of whom I said, 'He who comes after me ranks ahead of me because he was before me" (John 1:15 NRSV).

While Jesus was born after John, He actually existed before him.

Later, John the Baptist said.

> This is the One I told you about: 'After me comes a man who has surpassed me, because He existed before me' (John 1:30 HCSB).

While strictly speaking, this does not mean that Jesus Christ was eternal, it is consistent with the idea of His eternal existence.

The writer to the Hebrews said that God the Son made the universe—as well as everything which is in it. He said.

> Long ago God spoke many times and in many ways to our ancestors through the prophets. But now in these final days, he has spoken to us through his Son. God promised everything to the Son as an inheritance, and through the Son he made the universe and everything in it (Hebrews 1:1,2 NLT).

God the Son created the universe. This is another indication of His eternal existence.

7. JESUS IS GOD THE SON, A MEMBER OF THE TRINITY

Jesus Christ is God the Son, the Second Person of the Trinity. It is important to realize that what is true about God is also true about each Person in the Trinity. The Bible says that God has existed for all eternity. The psalmist wrote.

> Before the mountains were brought forth, or ever you had formed the earth and the world, from everlasting to everlasting you are God (Psalm 90:2 NRSV).

Since eternal existence is an attribute of God alone, it logically follows that Jesus, being God has existed for all eternity.

This means that there was no point when He came into existence. Since He had no beginning, He will have no end. He is not limited by time in any sense. Of course, this characteristic or attribute belongs to God alone.

8. JESUS IS EQUAL TO GOD IN HIS NAMES

Jesus is also spoken of as an equal with God. They both possess the same names. We can make the following observations.

A. JESUS IS THE "I AM"

At the famous encounter at the "burning bush," the God of the Bible told Moses that He was the "I am." We read.

> God replied, "I AM THE ONE WHO ALWAYS IS. Just tell them, 'I AM has sent me to you'" (Exodus 3:14 NLT).

Therefore, the God of the Bible says that He is the "I Am."

Jesus applied this same title to Himself. In the Gospel of John, we read of Jesus making this claim when addressing the religious rulers.

> "Your father Abraham rejoiced to see My day, and he saw it and was glad." Then the Jews said to Him, "You are not yet fifty years old, and have You seen Abraham?" Jesus said to them, "Most assuredly, I say to you, before Abraham was, I AM" (John 8:56-58 NKJV).

The fact that the people understood His claim can be seen in their reaction. Scripture says they attempted to kill Him with stones when He made this statement.

> At this, they picked up stones to stone him, but Jesus hid himself, slipping away from the temple grounds (John 8:59 NIV).

They certainly understood who Jesus was claiming to be!

B. JESUS IS LORD

The God of the Bible is called "the LORD" in the Old Testament. We read in the Book of Exodus about this. It says.

> God also said to Moses, "I am the LORD. I appeared to Abraham, to Isaac and to Jacob as God Almighty, but by my name the LORD I did not make myself known to them" (Exodus 6:2,3 NIV).

The LORD is the personal name of God. It is the Hebrew "Yahweh."

Jesus is also addressed as LORD. On the Day of Pentecost, Peter said the following about Jesus to the crowd that had gathered.

> Therefore let all the house of Israel know with certainty that God has made this Jesus, whom you crucified, both Lord and Messiah! (Acts 2:36 HCSB).

Jesus' resurrection from the dead gives further proof that He is Lord.

Paul wrote that Jesus Christ is Lord, Yahweh.

> Therefore I want you to understand that no one speaking by the Spirit of God ever says "Let Jesus be cursed!" and no one can say "Jesus is Lord" except by the Holy Spirit (1 Corinthians 12:3 NRSV).

Jesus is the God of the Old Testament.

C. JESUS IS THE LORD OF LORDS

The God of the Old Testament is called LORD OF LORDS. Moses wrote the following.

> For the LORD your God is the God of gods and Lord of lords, the great, mighty, and awesome God, showing no partiality and taking no bribe (Deuteronomy 10:17 HCSB).

Jesus is also called the LORD OF LORDS. In the Book of Revelation, it says.

> They will go to war against the lamb. The lamb will conquer them because he is Lord of lords and King of kings. Those who are called, chosen, and faithful are with him" (Revelation 17:14 God's Word).

Both the God of the Old Testament, and Jesus Christ, are called the Lord of Lords.

D. JESUS IS THE SHEPHERD

The Lord is the shepherd of His people. David wrote in the famous 23rd Psalm.

> The LORD is my shepherd; I shall not want (Psalm 23:1 KJV).

The LORD, our Shepherd, meets all of our needs.

Jesus is also the Good Shepherd.

> I am the good shepherd. I know my own and my own know me, just as the Father knows me and I know the Father. And I lay down my life for the sheep (John 10:14,15 NRSV).

There is only one "Good Shepherd." It is the LORD.

E. JESUS IS THE ALPHA AND OMEGA

Alpha and omega are the first and last letters of the Greek alphabet. The Bible says that God alone is the Alpha and Omega. John wrote in the Book of Revelation about God claiming this for Himself.

> "I am the Alpha and the Omega," says the Lord God, "the One who is, who was, and who is coming, the Almighty" (Revelation 1:8 HCSB).

While the Lord God is the Alpha and Omega, we also discover that Jesus Christ is also the Alpha and Omega. Jesus said.

> I am the Alpha and the Omega, the First and the Last, the Beginning and the End. "Blessed are those who wash their robes, that they may have the right to the tree of life and may go through the gates into the city" (Revelation 22:12,13 NIV).

Therefore, we see that there are a large number of names that belong to God alone, that also belong to Jesus.

F. JESUS IS IMMANUEL: GOD WITH US

Jesus was to be called "Immanuel—God with us." We read about this in Matthew's gospel. He wrote.

> All this happened so that what the Lord had spoken through
> the prophet came true: "The virgin will become pregnant and
> give birth to a son, and they will name him Immanuel," which
> means "God is with us" (Matthew 1:22,23 God's Word).

The fact that Jesus is called, "God with us," is another indication of
His deity.

9. JESUS HAS A UNIQUE RELATIONSHIP WITH GOD THE FATHER

There is more indirect evidence for Jesus' deity. We find that He had a
unique relationship with God the Father. Indeed, He called God "My
Father."

> Jesus answered, "I do not have a demon, but I honor my
> Father, and you dishonor me" (John 8:49 ESV).

There is something else we must note. Jesus never equated His relationship with the Father with the relationship that His disciples had.
He never referred to the Father as "Our Father" when referring to His
relationship with God. It was always "Your Father" and "My Father."

For example, at His resurrection, He made this distinction to Mary
Magdalene. We read the following.

> Jesus said to her, "Do not hold on to me, because I have not
> yet ascended to the Father. But go to my brothers and say to
> them, 'I am ascending to my Father and your Father, to my
> God and your God'" (John 20:17 NRSV).

Therefore, Jesus was careful to make the distinction between His relationship with God the Father and that of others. Indeed, it was not the same.

JESUS AND THE FATHER ARE ONE

We find further statements from Jesus which illustrates this truth. He
said to the religious rulers.

I and my Father are one (John 10:30 KJV).

The religious leaders wanted to kill Jesus for making this statement—they knew He was claiming some type of equality with God. In fact, when they brought Him before Pontius Pilate they made clear their reason for wanting Jesus dead.

> The Jewish leaders replied, "By our laws he ought to die because he called himself the Son of God" (John 19:7 NLT).

They realized whom Jesus claimed to be. Though they did not believe His claims, they certainly understood what He was saying.

10. JESUS IS PUT ON AN EQUAL LEVEL WITH GOD

On a number of occasions Jesus is associated with the God of the Bible in an equal manner. For example, the baptismal formula in Scripture puts Jesus on an equal level with God the Father. We read.

> Go therefore and make disciples of all nations, baptizing them in the name of the Father and of the Son and of the Holy Spirit (Matthew 28:19 NRSV).

The Father, Son, and Holy Spirit are all equated in the baptismal formula.

We also find Jesus, along with the Holy Spirit, is equated with God the Father in the apostolic benediction. It says.

> The grace of the Lord Jesus Christ, the love of God, and the communion of the Holy Spirit be with all of you (2 Corinthians 13:14 NRSV).

Again, He is placed on an equal level with God the Father. Yet the Bible says that God shares His glory with nobody!

> I am the Lord! That is my name! I will not share my glory with anyone else, or the praise due me with idols (Isaiah 42:8 NET).

Since God will not share His glory with anyone, this is another indication of the deity of Christ. Indeed, He is God.

11. JESUS HAS A HEAVENLY ORIGIN

Scripture says that the origin of Jesus Christ was not from the earth but rather from heaven. The writer to the Hebrews compared the Old Testament character Melchizedek with Jesus. He made the comparison in this manner.

> Without father, without mother, without genealogy, having neither beginning of days nor end of life, but resembling the Son of God, he remains a priest forever (Hebrews 7:3 NRSV).

Melchizedek resembled God the Son. Scripture records no beginning and no end for him. As the eternal God, Jesus had no beginning and certainly He will have no end.

The Bible says that Jesus Christ came to earth from heaven. The Gospel of John records the words of John the Baptist.

> The one who comes from above is above all; the one who is from the earth belongs to the earth, and speaks as one from the earth. The one who comes from heaven is above all (John 3:31 NIV).

John testified of Jesus' heavenly origin.

Jesus Himself claimed that He came down from heaven to the earth. He said.

> For I have come down from heaven to do the will of God who sent me, not to do what I want (John 6:38 NLT).

According to the Bible, Jesus' origin was from heaven above. This is further testimony of His divine origin.

12. JESUS ALLOWED HIMSELF TO BE WORSHIPPED

The God who reveals Himself in the Bible has made it clear that He is the only One deserving worship. In the Ten Commandments He said.

You shall have no other gods before Me (Exodus 20:3 NKJV).

Worship belongs to God alone.

When Satan wanted Jesus to worship him, Jesus refused. Instead, He responded in the following way.

"Get out of here, Satan," Jesus told him. "For the Scriptures say, 'You must worship the Lord your God; serve only him'" (Matthew 4:10 NLT).

Worship belongs to God alone.

A. JESUS WAS WORSHIPPED BY THE PEOPLE

Jesus testified that worship is something that is reserved for God alone. Yet, Jesus allowed Himself to be worshiped.

And as they went, Jesus met them. "Greetings!" he said. And they ran to him, held his feet, and worshiped him (Matthew 28:9 NLT).

Jesus received their worship.

On another occasion, Scripture records someone saying the following words to Jesus.

Then he said, "Lord, I believe!" And he worshiped Him (John 9:38 NKJV).

Jesus allowed Himself to be worshiped on this occasion also. If only God is to be worshiped, as the Bible testifies, and Jesus allowed Himself to be worshiped, then the natural conclusion is that Jesus believed Himself to be God.

On another occasion, Jesus said.

> That all should honor the Son just as they honor the Father.
> He who does not honor the Son does not honor the Father
> who sent Him (John 5:23 NKJV).

Jesus said people were to honor Him "just as" they honor God the
Father. If Jesus were not God, then for people to honor Him, as they
honored God, would be blasphemous.

B. THE ANGELS WERE COMMANDED TO WORSHIP JESUS

The first chapter of Hebrews tells us that God commanded the angels
to worship Jesus. It reads as follows.

> For God never said to any angel what he said to Jesus: "You
> are my Son. Today I have become your Father." And again
> God said, "I will be his Father, and he will be my Son." And
> then, when he presented his honored Son to the world, God
> said, "Let all the angels of God worship him" (Hebrews 1:5,6
> NLT).

Since God the Father commanded worship of the Son, the Son must
be of equal character with the Father. Otherwise He would not give
that command.

C. ALL CREATION IS TO WORSHIP JESUS

We are told that all of creation will worship Jesus. John wrote about
this in the Book of Revelation. He put it this way.

> I heard every creature in heaven, on earth, under the earth,
> and on the sea. Every creature in those places was singing,
> "To the one who sits on the throne and to the lamb be praise,
> honor, glory, and power forever and ever." The four living
> creatures said, "Amen!" Then the leaders bowed and wor-
> shiped (Revelation 5:13,14 God's Word).

Jesus, "the Lamb," richly deserved the worship of all creation.

13. JESUS WAS ADDRESSED IN PRAYER

Jesus was also directly addressed in prayer. We find that the Apostles specifically asked Jesus who should replace Judas.

> Then they prayed, "Lord, you know everyone's heart. Show us which of these two you have chosen" (Acts 1:24 NIV).

We only pray to God, nobody else.

Stephen, the first recorded martyr of the Christian church, prayed directly to Jesus as he was being killed by an unruly mob. He said.

> While they were stoning Stephen, he prayed, "Lord Jesus, receive my spirit." Then he knelt down and cried out in a loud voice, "Lord, do not hold this sin against them." When he had said this, he died (Acts 7:59,60 NRSV).

Only God is addressed in prayer. Jesus, therefore, must be God.

14. JESUS FORGAVE SINS

Another indirect testimony to Jesus being God is His ability to forgive sins. In the presence of the religious leaders, Jesus told a sinful woman that her sins were forgiven.

> Then He said to her, "Your sins are forgiven" (Luke 7:48 NKJV).

He claimed to be able to forgive sins.

On another occasion, He said the following to a paralyzed man.

> My son, your sins are forgiven (Mark 2:5 NLT).

The religious rulers, on each of these occasions, were indignant. They demanded an explanation as to why Jesus would speak in this manner.

Why would he say such a thing? He must think he is God!
Only God can forgive sins (Mark 2:7 CEV).

No doubt the rulers were remembering what God had previously said.

I, I am He who blots out your transgressions for my own sake,
and I will not remember your sins (Isaiah 43:25 NRSV).

If only God has the ability to forgive sins, and Jesus claimed the ability
to forgive sins, then Jesus is claiming to be God. Humans may tempo-
rarily forgive sins committed against other humans, but only God can
eternally forgive sins. By claiming to forgive sins Jesus demonstrated
His deity.

There is something else. Jesus forgave sins that were committed against
the Lord God. Only God has the right to forgive sins against Him.
We can only forgive sins that have been committed against us. This is
another indication that Jesus is God.

15. JESUS WILL JUDGE THE WORLD

Judgment of the world is something that only God can do. The Bible
says the following about God judging the earth.

Let the fields be jubilant, and everything in them. Then all
the trees of the forest will sing for joy; they will sing before
the LORD, for he comes, he comes to judge the earth. He
will judge the world in righteousness and the peoples in his
truth (Psalm 96:12,13 NIV).

The Lord will come and judge the earth.

Jesus claimed that He would judge the world. We read in John's gospel.

For the Father judges no one, but has committed all judgment to the Son (John 5:22 NKJV).

The Son will be judge of the world.

The Apostle Paul said that God will judge the entire world through Jesus. Before a hostile crowd in Athens, Paul said the following about Jesus.

> Because He has set a day on which He is going to judge the world in righteousness by the Man He has appointed. He has provided proof of this to everyone by raising Him from the dead (Acts 17:31 HCSB).

According to Paul, Jesus will be the One whom every human being will have to answer to.

Paul wrote to Timothy about Jesus judging the world.

> In the presence of God and of Christ Jesus, who will judge the living and the dead, and in view of his appearing and his kingdom, I give you this charge (2 Timothy 4:1 NIV).

The Bible says that only God has the right to judge the world—no one else has that authority. However, it also says that Jesus claimed that He would be that judge. This is more indirect evidence that Jesus is God.

16. JESUS IS THE CREATOR

Among the many deeds attributed to Jesus is the creation of the entire universe. The Scripture expressly states that Jesus was involved as the Creator. The Gospel of John, in speaking of Jesus, said.

> All things were made by him; and without him was not anything made that was made (John 1:3 KJV).

Here we have the statement that Jesus created everything. Not one thing has been created apart from Him.

The Apostle Paul also testified to Jesus being the Creator. He wrote of this aspect of Jesus' character to the church at Colosse.

> For all things in heaven and on earth were created by him- all things, whether visible or invisible, whether thrones or dominions, whether principalities or powers—all things were created through him and for him (Colossians 1:16 NET).

This statement makes it abundantly clear that Jesus created all things in the universe. This includes all things visible and invisible.

Though Jesus was the Creator of all things, this world did not recognize Him as such. One of the saddest verses in the Bible testifies to that fact.

> He was in the world, and the world was made by him, and the world knew him not (John 1:10 KJV).

Jesus created the world. However, when He visited His creation the people did not receive Him for who He truly was. This, of course, is tragic.

17. JESUS SUSTAINS ALL THINGS BY HIS SPOKEN WORD

Not only did Jesus create everything in the beginning, He also sustains His creation. The Apostle Paul, after testifying to the creative work of Jesus, wrote.

> He himself is before all things and all things are held together in him (Colossians 1:17 NET).

All things are held together by Christ.

The Book of Hebrews takes this a step further. It teaches that Christ is "upholding all things by his powerful word."

> The Son is the radiance of his glory and the representation of his essence, and he sustains all things by his powerful word (Hebrews 1:3 NET).

The New Living Translation puts it this way.

The Son reflects God's own glory, and everything about him represents God exactly. He sustains the universe by the mighty power of his command (Hebrews 1:3 NLT).

Jesus is the One who holds the universe together. That is, He is the Person who keeps it running in an orderly fashion. The idea is that Jesus is keeping all things together by His spoken Word.

Thus, it is the spoken word of Jesus that now upholds the universe. This testifies to the magnificent power which He possesses.

18. JESUS IS THE RULER OVER ALL THINGS

The Apostle Paul testified that Jesus Christ is the ruler over all things in the universe. He said to the Colossians.

And you have been filled in him, who is the head over every ruler and authority (Colossians 2:10 NET).

Jesus rules the universe, and all that is in it. Therefore, Jesus Christ is both Creator and Ruler.

19. JESUS WILL RAISE THE DEAD

Scripture teaches that Jesus Christ will raise the dead, as well as transform the bodies of believers. John records the Lord saying.

Do not be amazed at this, for a time is coming when all who are in their graves will hear his voice and come out—those who have done good will rise to live, and those who have done evil will rise to be condemned (John 5:28,29 NIV).

These are tremendous claims which Jesus has made of Himself.

The Apostle Paul also wrote about Jesus raising the dead when He returns. He explained what will happen in his letter to the Philippians.

He will take these weak mortal bodies of ours and change them into glorious bodies like his own, using the same mighty power that he will use to conquer everything, everywhere (Philippians 3:21 NLT).

Since only God has the power to raise the dead, this is another indication that Jesus Christ is indeed God Almighty.

20. JESUS GIVES LIFE TO WHOMEVER HE PLEASES

The Bible says that Jesus has the authority to grant life to whomever He pleases. Jesus Himself said.

Just as the Father raises the dead and gives life, so the Son gives life to anyone he wants to (John 5:21 CEV).

Both the Father and the Son have authority to give life to believers. This puts the Father and Jesus on an equal level.

21. JESUS WILL GIVE ETERNAL LIFE TO BELIEVERS

Jesus said that He will give eternal life to those who believe in Him. John records Jesus saying the following.

I give them eternal life, and they will never perish. No one will snatch them out of my hand (John 10:28 NRSV).

He is the One who grants life everlasting. Again, we have another fantastic claim by Jesus.

When Jesus prayed to God the Father, He again acknowledged He was able to do this. John records Jesus saying to the Father.

For you have given him authority over everyone in all the earth. He gives eternal life to each one you have given him (John 17:2 NLT).

This is another indication of Jesus' deity.

22. EVERYONE WILL CONFESS THAT JESUS IS LORD

The Scripture says that everything in heaven, earth, and under the earth will confess that Jesus Christ is Lord. The Apostle emphasized this in his letter to the Philippians. He said.

> This is why God has given him an exceptional honor—the name honored above all other names—so that at the name of Jesus everyone in heaven, on earth, and in the world below will kneel and confess that Jesus Christ is Lord to the glory of God the Father. (Philippians 2:9-11 God's Word).

The fact that everything in the universe will confess Jesus is Lord (Yahweh) proves that He indeed is Almighty God.

23. JESUS HAS EQUAL GLORY WITH GOD THE FATHER

Jesus claimed equal glory with God the Father.

> So now, Father, glorify me in your own presence with the glory that I had in your presence before the world existed (John 17:5 NRSV).

Only God could claim that. He shares His glory with no one. We read in Isaiah.

> I am doing this for myself, only for myself. Why should my name be dishonored? I will not give my glory to anyone else (Isaiah 48:11 God's Word).

Since God shares His glory with no other, Jesus must be God.

24. HE HAS THE SAME NATURE AS GOD

Scripture says that Jesus has the same nature as the God of the Bible.

> In your relationships with one another, have the same mind-set as Christ Jesus: Who, being in very nature God, did not

consider equality with God something to be used to his own advantage (Philippians 2:5,6 NIV).

The writer to the Hebrews said that Jesus is the exact representation of God.

> The Son is the radiance of God's glory and the exact representation of his being, sustaining all things by his powerful word (Hebrews 1:3 NIV).

Jesus is God by nature.

THE CLAIMS ARE NOT ENOUGH

If God did reveal Himself to humanity, then we would expect Him to identify Himself as God. However, we would expect more than mere claims. They would have to be backed up with a demonstration of His power and knowledge. Jesus realized that claiming to be God does not, by itself, make the claims true. He said.

> If I testify about Myself, My testimony is not valid (John 5:31 HCSB).

This is why Jesus did more than make claims about Himself. He backed it up with His works. He said.

> But I have a testimony greater than John's. The works that the Father has given me to complete, the very works that I am doing, testify on my behalf that the Father has sent me. And the Father who sent me has himself testified on my behalf. You have never heard his voice or seen his form, and you do not have his word abiding in you, because you do not believe him whom he has sent (John 5:36-38 NRSV).

He backed up His claims with convincing evidence. These evidences include miracles, fulfilled prophecy, and His resurrection from the dead. All of the evidence points to the fact that Jesus Christ is more than a mere man. Indeed, He is the Almighty God.

SUMMARY TO QUESTION 6
DOES THE BIBLE INDIRECTLY TEACH THAT JESUS IS GOD?

The Bible makes it clear that Jesus Christ was fully human. However, Scripture gives evidence, both directly and indirectly, that Jesus Christ was more than a mere man. From the description of Jesus as recorded in the New Testament, we find that He is the eternal God. We have the following indirect evidences that Jesus is the God of the Bible.

For one thing, we find that Jesus possesses a number of attributes or characteristics that belong to deity. Indeed, Scripture says that Jesus has existed from all eternity. Only God is eternal in nature.

Scripture teaches that Jesus is also a member of the Holy Trinity. In fact, we find that He is put on an equal level with God the Father and God the Holy Spirit. This would never happen unless Jesus was God Himself.

Jesus Christ is also equal to God in certain names. There are names such as King of Kings, Lord of Lords, and the Good Shepherd belong to God alone. Yet they are also given to Jesus. This is another factor in demonstrating that they are equal in nature.

We also find that while on earth Jesus had a unique relationship with God the Father. He could address Him as "My Father" in a unique way from other people. In fact, Jesus never equated His relationship with the Father as being the same as others. His was different.

The Bible also emphasizes Jesus had a heavenly origin. In fact, His origin is contrasted with human beings whose origin is from the earth.

One clear mark of deity is that Jesus Christ allowed Himself to be worshiped. Worship is something which is due to God alone. The fact the Father commanded the angels to worship Jesus, as well as the fact that He received it, goes to show that Jesus is God Himself.

There is also the fact that Jesus was addressed in prayer. Only God is addressed in prayer. We do not pray to angels or to other humans.

Of all the indirect references that shows that Jesus is God, one of the strongest is His claim to forgive sins. In the Old Testament, the God of the Bible makes it clear that He alone has the right to forgive sins. The New Testament records that Jesus claimed the same right. Jesus would not make this claim unless He had the authority to do so.

Jesus also claimed to be the judge of the world. Other New Testament writers echoed His claim. Since Scripture is clear that the judgment of humanity belongs to God alone—the logical inference is that Jesus is the God of Scripture.

The Bible also says that Jesus is the Creator of the entire universe. Furthermore, He sustains the universe by His spoken word. Jesus also presently rules the universe. Therefore, the creation, and the running of the universe, belong to Him.

We also find that Jesus will raise the dead at His coming. Again, He claimed this right for Himself. Since only God can raise the dead, Jesus must Himself be God.

Jesus gives spiritual life as well as eternal life to believers. This is something which only God can grant. No human, angel, or any other created being, can impart life.

The Apostle Paul wrote that everyone will one day confess Jesus Christ as LORD. This means they will acknowledge Him as Yahweh.

The New Testament also says that Jesus has equal glory with God the Father. Since God will not share His glory with anyone, the conclusion is that Jesus is God Himself.

In addition, Jesus performs work that only God can perform. These abilities cannot be delegated because they are characteristics of God alone.

We conclude that the Bible indirectly teaches in a number of different ways that Jesus Christ is Almighty God—the Second Person of the Holy Trinity.

QUESTION 7

Why Was Jesus Called
Immanuel? (God With Us)

There is a word used of Jesus whose meaning has puzzled many people. In Matthew's gospel, Jesus is called "Immanuel."

> The virgin will conceive and give birth to a son, and they will call him "Immanuel" (which means "God with us (Matthew 1:23 NIV).

When Scripture says they shall name Him Immanuel, does this mean that it is His personal name? Should we call Him this instead of Jesus?

Actually this passage is not giving a new name, or a personal name, to Jesus. The fact that Jesus was born is a fulfillment of Bible prophecy. We read the following prediction in Isaiah.

> Therefore the Lord himself will give you a sign: The virgin will conceive and give birth to a son, and will call him Immanuel (Isaiah 7:14 NIV).

The fulfillment is not in the naming of the child Jesus, but rather in the entire account of His life and ministry. It is not that Jesus ever bore the name Immanuel. He did not. The name indicates His role. Jesus is the One who brought God's presence to humanity.

Matthew explains to his readers what this phrase means. It is actually a transliteration of four small Hebrew words into Greek. When the Hebrew words are joined together the sound is "Immanuel."

Therefore, this word used by Matthew is not a name for Jesus, it is rather a statement about the fulfillment of Isaiah's prophecy. God is now with us!

GOD IS WITH US BECAUSE OF JESUS

Consequently, it is a statement about Jesus, it is not a proper name, nor is it a prayer. Matthew's use of this term may be understood in one of two ways. They are as follows.

OPTION 1: IT DESCRIBES JESUS' COMING

The phrase "God is with us" describes the coming of Jesus. He is God who has become a human. Therefore, this one phrase is a mini summary of Jesus' purpose of arriving on the earth. Indeed, He is God who became one of us. John wrote.

> No one has ever seen God. The One and Only Son—the One who is at the Father's side—He has revealed Him (John 1:18 HCSB).

God the Son came to this earth to let us know what the living God is like. Jesus is the One who explained Him. In that sense, He is "God with us."

OPTION 2: IT DESCRIBES GOD'S GRACE BY SENDING THE MESSIAH

There is a second option. Matthew may have wanted to show that the virgin conception was not something new, but that it had been predicted by the prophet Isaiah.

Therefore, "God is with us" would not so much describe the exact nature of Jesus coming to the world, but rather that God has been gracious to His people by sending His Messiah. In other words, God keeps His promises. He is still with His people.

In whatever way of these two ways that we understand this description of Jesus, it is consistent with the teaching of the remainder of the New

Testament. Indeed, God became a human being in Jesus Christ. In doing so, He showed that He was still with the people of the nation of Israel. In this sense, it could truly have been said by the people of Jesus' day that "God is with us."

SUMMARY TO QUESTION 7
WHY WAS JESUS CALLED IMMANUEL? (GOD WITH US)

When the conception of Jesus was announced to Joseph the angel told him that a Son would be born who would be called "Immanuel" – "God with us." Does this mean that Immanuel is the personal name of Jesus?

It does not. It is actually a transliteration of a number of Hebrew words which translated means "God with us." Therefore, Jesus is not to be called "Immanuel." Indeed, this name is never used of Him in the New Testament.

It likely is emphasizing one of two things.

The phrase may be highlighting the truth of the gospel that God became a human being in Jesus Christ. Indeed, the coming of Christ, God the Son, was for the purpose of explaining God to the human race. "God with us" is a mini summary of His coming.

It is also possible that Matthew is emphasizing that God was faithful to His promises in sending the Messiah to His people, the Jews. In other words, God is with us in the fact that He always keeps His word.

In sum, when the conception of Jesus was announced to Joseph, the angel told him that a Son would be born to Mary who would be called Immanuel—God with us. The phrase may be emphasizing the truth of the gospel—that God became a human being in Jesus Christ.

It is also possible that Matthew is emphasizing that God was faithful to His promises in sending the Messiah to His people, the Jews. Either way, it is consistent with the idea that God became a human being in the Person of Jesus Christ.

What Does Jesus' Preexistence Mean?

The doctrine of Jesus' preexistence means that He existed before He came to earth as a human being. There are a number of passages that make this biblical truth clear. We can note the various passages as follows.

1. JESUS EXISTED BEFORE ABRAHAM

When talking to the religious leaders of His day, Jesus said that he existed before the patriarch Abraham. His profound words are recorded by John.

> Jesus said to them, "I assure you: Before Abraham was, I am" (John 8:58 HCSB).

Before Abraham was born, Jesus existed.

2. JESUS HAS EXISTED ETERNALLY

One of the key New Testament verses says Jesus existed in the beginning with God. John begins his gospel by stating this fact. He put it this way.

> In the beginning was the Word, and the Word was with God, and the Word was God (John 1:1 KJV).

Not only did Jesus exist before Abraham, He has existed eternally. This is the consistent testimony of Scripture.

3. JESUS IS PREEMINENT OVER ALL CREATION

The Apostle Paul also said that Jesus Christ was preeminent over all creation. He wrote the following to the Colossians.

> The Son is the image of the invisible God, the firstborn over all creation (Colossians 1:15 NIV).

In this context, the word translated "firstborn" has the idea of preeminence. Jesus as the Creator has authority over all of His creation.

4. JESUS HAD PAST GLORY

While here upon the earth, Jesus Himself spoke about His past glory with God the Father. On the night of His betrayal, our Lord prayed the following to Him.

> Now, Father, glorify Me in Your presence with that glory I had with You before the world existed (John 17:5 HCSB).

According to the words of Jesus, He was in the presence of God the Father before this world was created. We do not exactly know what this glory consisted of. Yet, we know this glory belongs to God alone.

Later in the prayer to His Father, Jesus spoke of the love the Father had for the Son before the world was made.

> Father, I want those you have given to me to be with me, to be where I am. I want them to see my glory, which you gave me because you loved me before the world was made (John 17:24 God's Word).

The fact that the Father loved the Son before the world was created is another indication that Jesus was in the presence of the Father before anything—whether angels, other heavenly beings, or humans, were created.

5. JESUS TOOK THE FORM OF A SERVANT

The Apostle Paul wrote about the coming of Jesus to the earth as taking the form of a servant, or a slave. He wrote the following to the Philippians.

> Who, being in very nature God, did not consider equality with God something to be used to his own advantage; rather, he made himself nothing by taking the very nature of a servant, being made in human likeness (Philippians 2:6,7 NIV).

Therefore, the One who existed as God for all eternity, came to this earth and took the form of a servant. God the Son humbled Himself for the purpose of saving humanity.

In sum, the Bible teaches that before anything was made, the Son of God, Jesus Christ, existed in the presence of God the Father.

SUMMARY TO QUESTION 8
WHAT DOES JESUS' PREEXISTENCE MEAN?

One of the key doctrines of the New Testament is the "preexistence of Jesus Christ." The existence of Jesus Christ did not begin when He was born as a babe in Bethlehem. Indeed, Jesus' preexistence means that He existed before He came to earth. The evidence is as follows.

Jesus told the religious rulers of His day that He existed before Abraham—a man who lived two thousand years earlier. While this does not necessarily mean that He existed eternally, the idea that Jesus was alive before Abraham is certainly consistent with this idea.

However, the Bible goes further than this. The Bible speaks of Jesus not only existed before Abraham, He has existed for all eternity. Indeed,

John begins His gospel by saying that the Word, Jesus, was in the beginning with God.

John then goes on to explain how the eternal God became a human being. The Lord Jesus, God the Son, came to earth to tell us who God is, as well as what He expects from us.

The Apostle Paul wrote of Jesus' position. His position is of one of preeminence over all creation. He rules over it.

Scripture also speaks of His previous glory. Jesus, in praying to God the Father, spoke of His time with the Father before the world was formed.

Jesus laid aside that glory when He came to earth as a human and took the role of a servant. Scripture emphasizes that He did this on our behalf.

This sums up what Scripture has to say about Jesus' preexistence. The point of all of this is that His existence did not begin as a babe in Bethlehem. Indeed, He has existed as God the Son for all eternity.

What Did Jesus Do Before He Came To Earth?

The Bible teaches that Jesus, God the Son, existed before He came to earth as a human being. Scripture also tells us some of the things that He did before He became human. We can list them as follows.

1. HE WAS THE CREATOR OF THE UNIVERSE

The Bible says that Jesus was the Creator of the entire universe. John wrote the following about this in his gospel. He said.

> All things were created through Him, and apart from Him not one thing was created that has been created (John 1:3 HCSB).

Note that all things were made by Him. Jesus, therefore, is the Creator.

The Apostle Paul wrote about Jesus being the one who created "all things." He wrote the following to the Colossians.

> Everything was created by him, everything in heaven and on earth, everything seen and unseen, including all forces and powers, and all rulers and authorities. All things were created by God's Son, and everything was made for him (Colossians 1:16 CEV).

The entire universe was made by Him. The writer to the Hebrews echoes this truth.

> In the past God spoke to our ancestors through the prophets at many times and in various ways, but in these last days he has spoken to us by his Son, whom he appointed heir of all things, and through whom also he made the universe (Hebrew 1:1-2 NIV).

Jesus was the Creator.

2. JESUS PRESERVED THE UNIVERSE AFTER HE CREATED IT

There is something else that we learn from the Bible. Jesus Christ, God the Son, not only created the universe, He also preserved His creation. Paul also wrote about this to the Colossians.

> He existed before everything else began, and he holds all creation together (Colossians 1:17 NLT).

He is the One who holds everything in the universe together. In other words, the reason as to why all things are held together is because of Jesus Christ! This is quite a claim.

The writer to the Hebrews takes this a step further. He says that all things in the universe are actually held together by His powerful Word. We read.

> The Son is the radiance of God's glory and the exact representation of his being, sustaining all things by his powerful word. After he had provided purification for sins, he sat down at the right hand of the Majesty in heaven (Hebrews 1:3 NIV).

Jesus' work of preservation continues until today.

In sum, we find at least two important things which Jesus did before He came to earth. First, He created all things. Second, He sustained that which He created. In fact, He continues to sustain the universe to this day.

SUMMARY TO QUESTION 9
WHAT DID JESUS DO BEFORE HE CAME TO EARTH?

God the Son, Jesus Christ, has been God from all eternity. The Bible makes it clear that Jesus did not have His origin as a babe in Bethlehem. Scripture also tells us about some of the things which He did before coming to earth.

Indeed, we find that He was certainly not inactive before He became a human being and lived among us. Two things are emphasized.

First, Jesus was the Creator of the entire universe. In other words, before He came to the earth He was busy creating all things.

Not only has God the Son created all things, He upholds His creation through His powerful word. All things in the universe are held together through the Word of God the Son. He is the force which has kept all things running intact. He continues to preserve the universe to this day.

Consequently, we find Him active before He came to earth as a human being.

Does The Fact That Jesus Received Worship Prove That He Is God?

In a number of instances, in the four gospels, we find people worshipping Jesus as Lord. For example, a blind man that Jesus healed said the following to Him.

> Lord, I believe. And he worshipped him (John 9:38 KJV).

This verse seems to clearly imply that people worshipped Jesus because they recognized He was God Himself. Other accounts record something similar.

IT DOES NOT NECESSARILY IMPLY DEITY

Do these accounts of Jesus receiving worship prove that He is deity? That He is God? Not necessarily. The Greek word that is translated, "worship" can have the idea of respect. It does not necessarily mean the worship of deity. A number of observations need to be made as we look at what the New Testament has to say.

1. THE INCIDENT WITH THE LEPER: IT WAS MORE LIKELY RESPECT THAN WORSHIP

The Bible says that a leper approached Jesus and asked for healing. Matthew records what happened as follows.

> When Jesus had come down from the mountain, great crowds followed him; and there was a leper who came to him and knelt before him, saying, "Lord, if you choose, you can make me clean" (Matthew 8:1,2 NRSV).

In this context, the leper bowed before Jesus. The word Greek translated, "bow the knee" or "knelt" is translated as "worship" in other contexts. In fact, some Bible translations render the word as "worship," here in Matthew. It is doubtful, however, that the leper was worshipping Jesus in the same way that he worshipped God. In this context, he seems to be coming to Jesus more out of respect than out of adoration.

2. JESUS DID RECEIVE THE WORSHIP OF THE CROWD

In the certain contexts, the worship of Jesus does show that He is God. When Jesus entered Jerusalem on Palm Sunday the crowds worshipped Him. Again, we read what happened in Matthew's gospel.

> When the chief priests and the scribes saw the amazing miracles he performed and the children shouting in the temple courtyard, "Hosanna to the Son of David!" they were irritated. They said to him, "Do you hear what these children are saying?" Jesus replied, "Yes, I do. Have you never read, 'From the mouths of little children and infants, you have created praise'?" (Matthew 21:15,16 God's Word).

The quotation was from Psalm 8:2. This part of the psalm is addressed to the Lord Himself. It describes the worship that He alone deserves. It says the following.

> Our Lord and Ruler, your name is wonderful everywhere on earth! You let your glory be seen in the heavens above. With praises from children and from tiny infants, you have built a fortress. It makes your enemies silent, and all who turn against you are left speechless (Psalm 8:1-2 CEV).

By applying this Psalm to Jesus, it indicates that He is worthy of worship—He is the Lord.

3. THE ANGELS WERE COMMANDED TO WORSHIP JESUS

The Bible says that the angels were commanded to worship God the Son, Jesus Christ, when He came into the world. We read of this in the Book of Hebrews. It says.

> And again, when he brings the firstborn into the world, he says, "Let all God's angels worship him" (Hebrews 1:6 ESV).

This is an illustration of the worship of the Son which is commanded by God the Father. If the God the Father commanded worship of the Son, then we should follow His command.

4. HE IS THE LORD OF GLORY

The Apostle Paul ascribes glory to the Lord Jesus. This would refer to the Shekinah, or heavenly, glory that belongs to God alone.

> The Lord will rescue me from every evil work and will bring me safely into His heavenly kingdom. To Him be the glory forever and ever! Amen (2 Timothy 4:18 HCSB).

Jesus has the same glory that belongs to God alone.

5. ALL WILL WORSHIP JESUS SOMEDAY

The Apostle Paul says that someday everyone will worship Jesus. He wrote the following to the Philippians.

> So that at the name of Jesus every knee will bow - in heaven and on earth and under the earth - and every tongue confess that Jesus Christ is Lord to the glory of God the Father (Philippians 2:10,11 NET).

The living God alone deserves our worship. Jesus Christ, as God the Son, is truly deserving of our worship.

SUMMARY TO QUESTION 10
DOES THE FACT THAT JESUS RECEIVED WORSHIP PROVE THAT HE IS GOD?

As God the Son, Jesus Christ rightfully received worship during His time here on the earth. In fact, Scripture specifically says that Jesus was worshipped. Indeed, we find a number of instances where this occurred.

However, we must be careful about concluding that all of the instances when people bowed down to Him prove that they acknowledged Him as God. In many cases, it is clear that He is worshipped as the one, true God. Yet, the word translated, "worship" can also be a term of respect.

In some contexts, we should understand the people giving Jesus great respect—rather than worship as God. Indeed, there a number of occasions when worship of Jesus was more of giving Him the due respect He deserved.

However, there is no indication that the people thought they were bowing down to God Himself. While this is what they were actually doing, there is nothing in the context which tells us they knew Jesus' true identity.

Therefore, each instance of the use of the word *worship*, when it is directly toward Jesus, needs to be decided on the context.

What we do know is this. Jesus Christ is the Lord of glory whom everyone, believer and unbeliever alike, will one day acknowledge. Indeed, the Bible says that every knee will bow and every tongue will confess that Jesus Christ is indeed Lord. All creation will worship Him!

QUESTION 11

Why Was Jesus Called The Word Of God? (Logos)

One of the titles of Jesus was the "Word" of God, the "*Logos*." We find it used several places in Scripture of Jesus—though only in the writings of John.

In the introduction to John's gospel we read the following.

> In the beginning was the word [logos], and the word [logos], was with God, and the word [logos], was God (John 1:1 KJV).

Here we are told that the "word," or "Logos," was with God, and that the Logos was God.

John also wrote how the Word, the Logos, became a human being. He said.

> So the Word [logos], became human and lived here on earth among us. He was full of unfailing love and faithfulness. And we have seen his glory, the glory of the only Son of the Father (John 1:14 NLT).

The Logos became a human being at a certain point in time.

In the Book of Revelation, it says the following about the Logos—the Word of God.

He is clothed in a robe dipped in blood, and the name by which he is called is The Word of God (Revelation 19:13 ESV).

Jesus is thus called "the Logos," the "Word of God."

THIS TERM LOGOS IS NOT DEFINED IN SCRIPTURE

While Jesus is called the "Logos," the term is never explained in Scripture. Although there is no explanation given in Scripture as to why Jesus is called the Word of God, there have been several suggested reasons.

1. IT MAY REFER TO WISDOM PERSONIFIED

It has been argued that Jesus is the personification of wisdom as is described in Proverbs 5-8. This section begins by saying.

My son, pay attention to my wisdom, listen well to my words of insight (Proverbs 5:1 NIV).

If this is the case, then Jesus personifies wisdom. He is perfect wisdom in everything that He said, and everything that He did. Whether or not this is what the word logos actually means when used in the New Testament, this is certainly true of Jesus.

2. THE WORD IS GOD'S COMMUNICATION TO HUMANITY

It is possible that the term "word" is used the same manner as does the Old Testament—it is the communication of God to humanity. This is exactly what Jesus did. Indeed, He revealed to the world the Word of God. Jesus is clearly the personification of the written and spoken Word.

In the Old Testament, God revealed His Word through the prophets, while in the New Testament, the Word of God was revealed in a Person—God the Son.

The writer to the Hebrews emphasized that Jesus was God's ultimate revelation to the human race. He wrote.

> In the past God spoke to our ancestors at many different times and in many different ways through the prophets. In these last days he has spoken to us through his Son. God made his Son responsible for everything. His Son is the one through whom God made the universe. His Son is the reflection of God's glory and the exact likeness of God's being. He holds everything together through his powerful words. After he had cleansed people from their sins, he received the highest position, the one next to the Father in heaven (Hebrews 1:1-3 God's Word).

Therefore, Jesus was God's Word, or communication, to lost humanity.

In sum, while we cannot be exactly certain what was meant by the Greek word logos, translated as "word," we have a couple of possibilities which fit well with the overall teaching of Scripture.

SUMMARY TO QUESTION 11
WHY WAS JESUS CALLED THE LOGOS?

In a few places in the New Testament, Jesus is called, "the Word of God." This term, which is only found in the writings of John, is not defined for us.

The first verse of John's gospel tells us that the Word, or the *logos*, was in the beginning with God. Later in the chapter, we are told that the Word became a human being. In the Book of Revelation, when Christ returns to the earth, we are told that His name is called the "Word of God."

Although Scripture does not define what is exactly meant by this term in these various contexts, there are a couple of suggested possibilities.

Some feel that the logos could refer to the fact that Jesus is the personification of wisdom. Wisdom is spoken of as something personal in the Book of Proverbs. Thus, this usage in John could refer back to what has been written in Proverbs.

There is also the suggestion that may refer to the fact that Jesus is God's communication to humanity. The testimony, or word, that God revealed through the prophets during the Old Testament period, was now made human with the coming of Christ. Hence the Word became flesh. Jesus, therefore, is the Living Word of God—now made known to us through the written Word of God.

While we may never be exactly certain what John meant by the term, we do know that these suggested meanings are in agreement with the overall teaching of Scripture on the subject of the Person of Jesus Christ. All wisdom is found in Him, and He is indeed the Living Word of God.

QUESTION 12

Was Jesus Called
The Son Of God?

Jesus of Nazareth was a human being. In fact, Scripture makes it clear that He had all the traits of a genuine human. However, He was much more than this.

Indeed, in the New Testament, this man Jesus is referred to as "the Son of God." His identity as the Son of God was recognized by God the Father, angels, as well as human beings.

We can make the following observations about the various people and groups which recognized Jesus of Nazareth as the Son of God.

1. THE TESTIMONY OF THE ANGEL GABRIEL TO JESUS' IDENTITY AS SON OF GOD

To begin with, we find the angels recognizing this fact. When announcing the upcoming birth of the child Jesus to Mary, the angel Gabriel said the child would be God's Son. Luke records his words to Mary as follows.

> And the angel answered her, "The Holy Spirit will come upon you, and the power of the Most High will overshadow you; therefore the child to be born will be called holy—the Son of God" (Luke 1:35 ESV).

Note that Jesus is to be called the "Son of God" according to the angel Gabriel. In other words, this is His title.

2. GOD THE FATHER RECOGNIZED JESUS AS HIS SON AS HE BEGAN HIS MINISTRY

As Jesus began His public ministry, we find that God the Father also acknowledged Jesus as His Son.

As soon as Jesus was baptized, he went up out of the water. At that moment heaven was opened, and he saw the Spirit of God descending like a dove and lighting on him. And a voice from heaven said, "This is my Son, whom I love; with him I am well pleased" (Matthew 3:16-17 NIV).

We also discover this to be true in another historical situation. At Jesus' transfiguration, the Father verbally acknowledged the Son before the prophets Moses and Elijah as well as Jesus' disciples Peter, James, and John. The Bible says.

He [Peter] was still speaking when a bright cloud overshadowed them. Then a voice came out of the cloud and said, "This is my Son, whom I love and with whom I am pleased. Listen to him!" (Matthew 17:5 God's Word).

Here Jesus is called the "Beloved Son," or the "Loved Son," by God the Father.

God the Father recognized Jesus as the Son of God, or God the Son. We read the following in the Book of Acts.

God made a promise to our ancestors. And we are here to tell you the good news that he has kept this promise to us. It is just as the second Psalm says about Jesus, "You are my son because today I have become your Father" (Acts 13:32-33 CEV).

Therefore, the Father specifically called Jesus "My son."

The writer to the Hebrews makes the same point. He says that when Jesus came into our world the Father called Jesus "His Son." It is stated in this manner.

For God never said to any angel what he said to Jesus: "You are my Son. Today I have become your Father." And again God said, "I will be his Father, and he will be my Son" (Hebrews 1:5 NLT).

This is a quotation from the Book of Psalms. Therefore, we have another reference of the Father recognizing the Son.

It is therefore clear from the New Testament that God the Father identified Jesus as God the Son.

3. THE CONFESSION OF PETER RECOGNIZED JESUS AS THE SON OF GOD

Not only did God the Father and the holy angels recognize Jesus as the Son, we find that humans did also. When Jesus asked His disciples whom they thought He was, Simon Peter, speaking for the group, testified that Jesus was the "Son of the living God." We read.

Simon Peter replied, "You are the Christ, the Son of the living God" (Matthew 16:16 ESV).

Simon Peter, therefore, recognized the true identity of Jesus of Nazareth. He was indeed the Son of God.

4. THE STATEMENTS OF JESUS AS TO HIS IDENTITY AS GOD'S SON

Not only did others recognize Jesus as God's Son, Jesus referred to Himself as the Son of God. John records Him saying the following.

I assure you: An hour is coming, and is now here, when the dead will hear the voice of the Son of God, and those who hear will live. (John 5:25 HCSB).

It is His voice, the voice of the Son of God, which will raise the dead.

In another place, John again records Jesus acknowledging that He is God the Son. At the death of His friend Lazarus we read the following.

When Jesus heard it, He said, "This sickness will not end in death but is for the glory of God, so that the Son of God may be glorified through it" (John 11:4 NIV).

According to Jesus, Lazarus' death was for the purpose of glorifying God the Son.

Later, John records that Jesus said it again. In another confrontation with the religious leaders, John records Jesus saying these words.

Do you say, 'You are blaspheming' to the One the Father set apart and sent into the world, because I said: I am the Son of God (John 10:36 HCSB).

It is clear that Jesus believed Himself to be the Son of God.

JESUS ACKNOWLEDGED HIS IDENTITY UNDER OATH

Jesus' understanding of His identity becomes even clearer at His trial. At Jesus' trial, while under oath, He admitted to being the Son of God. We read what happened.

But Jesus remained silent. Then the high priest said to him, "I demand in the name of the living God that you tell us whether you are the Messiah, the Son of God." Jesus replied, "Yes, it is as you say. And in the future you will see me, the Son of Man, sitting at God's right hand in the place of power and coming back on the clouds of heaven" (Matthew 26:63,64 NLT).

This removes all doubt as to what Jesus believed about His identity.

In fact, the charge that was brought to Pontius Pilate, by the religious rulers, is that Jesus claimed to be the Son of God. We read.

The Jewish leaders replied, "By our laws he ought to die because he called himself the Son of God" (John 19:7 NLT).

The religious leaders understood that Jesus was claiming equality with God. Indeed, this is one of the reasons as to why they wanted Him put to death. They considered His claim to be blasphemy.

Of course, it would have been blasphemy if it was not true. However, Jesus' claims about Himself were indeed true.

5. THE DEMONS RECOGNIZE JESUS AS THE SON OF GOD

The Bible says that it was not only the friends of Jesus who recognized His identity as the Son of God. There is another testimony from those who did not believe in Him. Indeed, the demons also recognized His identity. We read in Matthew.

> They began screaming at him, "Why are you bothering us, Son of God? You have no right to torture us before God's appointed time!" (Matthew 8:29 NLT).

They too, knew who Jesus was.

6. THE ROMAN CENTURION AT JESUS' CROSS RECOGNIZED HIS IDENTITY

We also find humans, who were not followers of Jesus, recognizing who He was. While Jesus was dying on the cross, the Roman centurion in charge of His crucifixion acknowledged Jesus' identity. Matthew writes.

> When the centurion and those with him, who were guarding Jesus, saw the earthquake and the things that had happened, they were terrified and said, "This man really was God's Son!" (Matthew 27:54 HCSB).

This Roman solider could see that Jesus was more than a mere man. Consequently, at Jesus' death this man publicly stated that Christ was God's Son.

Thus, we find during His public ministry, as to His identity as the Son of God, there was the testimony of those who believed in Him, as well as those who did not.

7. JOHN SAID JESUS IS THE SON OF GOD THE FATHER

After, Jesus' ascension into heaven, we read again of this truth. Indeed, Jesus is the "Son of God the Father" according to the Apostle John. He stated.

> Grace, mercy, and peace will be with us from God the Father and from Jesus Christ, the Son of the Father, in truth and love (2 John 3 HCSB).

Jesus is the Son of God the Father.

8. THE ACKNOWLEDGMENT OF THE APOSTLE PAUL

We also find that the Apostle Paul acknowledged Jesus' identity as the Son of God. He wrote the following words to church in the city of Rome.

> From Paul, a servant of Jesus Christ, called to be an apostle and appointed to spread the Good News of God. (God had already promised this Good News through his prophets in the Holy Scriptures. This Good News is about his Son, our Lord Jesus Christ. In his human nature he was a descendant of David. In his spiritual, holy nature he was declared the Son of God. This was shown in a powerful way when he came back to life (Romans 1:1-4 God's Word).

Here Paul emphasizes that Jesus was shown, or declared to be, the "Son of God" in a powerful way when He came back from the dead.

Therefore, it is the united testimony of the New Testament that Jesus is the Son of God.

SUMMARY TO QUESTION 12
WAS JESUS CALLED THE SON OF GOD?

While Jesus of Nazareth was fully human, the New Testament also says that He is the Son of God. We have many different lines of testimony to this fact.

To begin with, the angel Gabriel, at the announcement of His conception, made it clear that the child Jesus was God's Son. Therefore, before He was even conceived He was acknowledged as God the Son.

God the Father acknowledged Jesus as the Son as soon as He began His public ministry. At Jesus' baptism, the voice of God the Father was heard to designate Him as the Beloved Son of the Father.

During Jesus' ministry, the Father again publicly acknowledged the Son at His Transfiguration. That the Father recognized the Son is also recorded for us in the Book of Acts, as well as the letter to the Hebrews.

Human beings also recognized Jesus as the Son. When Jesus asked His disciples whom they thought He was, Simon Peter, speaking for the group, acknowledged that Jesus was the Son of God. This confession of Peter was acknowledged by Jesus. He truly is the Son of God.

This brings us to our next point. Jesus Himself testified to His identity as the Son of God. The four gospels, on a number of occasions, record Him claiming to be God the Son. Therefore, we have Jesus own testimony as to His identity. Furthermore, at His trial before the religious rulers, Jesus acknowledged under oath that He was the Son of God.

Interestingly, we also have the testimony of those who were not believers in Jesus as to His identity as the Son of God. During His earthly ministry, the demons publicly acknowledged Jesus. They knew who He was.

At the time of His death on the cross, the Roman centurion publicly stated that the man whom He was watching being crucified was actually the Son of God.

Therefore, we have the testimony of His identity from those who did not believe in Him.

After Jesus ascended into heaven, the acknowledgments continued. We find that the Apostle John, in his second letter, testified that Jesus was the Father's Son.

In the writings of the Apostle Paul, there is the same truth taught. Indeed, Paul stressed that Jesus was declared to be the Son of God with power by His resurrection from the dead.

In sum, there is united testimony in the New Testament with respect to Jesus identity. He is God the Son. Of this, there is no doubt.

QUESTION 13

Are Others In Scripture, Apart From Jesus, Called The Son Of God Or Sons Of God?

Although Jesus is called the "Son of God," we also find this term applied to humans as well as other heavenly beings. Indeed, from a study of Scripture we find that the term "son of God" is applied to the first man Adam, created heavenly beings, Israel, those who make peace, and Christians. The evidence for this is as follows.

1. ADAM WAS A SON OF GOD

Adam, the first man whom God created, was called the "son of God." We read of this in Jesus' genealogy as recorded by Luke. It says.

> Kenan was the son of Enosh. Enosh was the son of Seth. Seth was the son of Adam. Adam was the son of God (Luke 3:38 NLT).

In this sense, Adam was a direct creation of God. In other words, he had no human father. Indeed, the Book of Genesis explains his creation in this manner.

> Then the LORD God formed the man out of the dust from the ground and breathed the breath of life into his nostrils, and the man became a living being (Genesis 2:7 HCSB).

Thus, Adam came into our world in a different manner than the rest of humanity.

2. ISRAEL WAS GOD'S SON

In the Old Testament, we find God saying that the nation Israel was His son. We read about this in Hosea. The Lord said.

> When Israel was a child, I loved him, and out of Egypt I called My son (Hosea 11:1 HCSB).

The nation had a special relationship with God the Father. Indeed, it was so special that the Lord referred to Israel as His "son."

3. CERTAINLY HEAVENLY BEINGS ARE THE SONS OF GOD

On at least one occasion in the Old Testament, heavenly beings which the Lord created are called "sons of God." In the Book of Job, we read the following.

> One day the sons of God came again to present themselves before the LORD, and Satan also came with them to present himself before the LORD (Job 2:1 HCSB).

"Sons" in this context, has nothing to do with a genetic relationship. They were created beings—all of whom were seemingly created at once.

4. THOSE WHO MAKE PEACE ARE GOD'S SONS

In the New Testament we are told that those who make peace are called the "sons of God." In the Sermon on the Mount, Jesus said.

> The peacemakers are blessed, for they will be called sons of God (Matthew 5:9 HCSB).

God wants us to be peacemakers—not merely peacekeepers. We bring people together—not keep them apart.

5. CHRISTIANS ARE CALLED GOD'S SONS

The designation "sons of God" is also used for Christians. We read the following statement of Jesus in Luke's gospel about the destiny of believers.

For they cannot die anymore, because they are like angels and are sons of God since they are sons of the resurrection (Luke 20:36 HCSB).

Some translations use the word "children" rather than sons. For example, the NIV reads.

And they can no longer die; for they are like the angels. They are God's children, since they are children of the resurrection (Luke 20:36 NIV).

Believers are God's sons, or God's children, through faith in Jesus Christ.

Therefore, we find that the term "son of God" is used a number of different ways in Scripture. It is not merely used as a designation for Jesus.

SUMMARY TO QUESTION 13
ARE OTHERS IN SCRIPTURE, APART FROM JESUS, CALLED THE SON OF GOD OR SONS OF GOD?

While Jesus Christ is called "the" Son of God in Scripture, He is not the only one with this designation. Indeed, we find this description used in a number of ways in the Bible.

Adam, the first human being whom God created, is called the "son of God" in Jesus' genealogy.

The nation Israel, in the Book of Hosea, is called "My son" by God. Therefore, Israel is a "son of God" in a special sense.

In the Book of Job, we are told that there was a time when certain created heavenly beings appeared before the Lord. They were designated the "sons of God." Therefore, this title can refer to these beings.

Jesus, in the Sermon on the Mount, said that those who are the peacemakers will be called the "sons of God." Therefore, this title can be used of those who bring people together for the purpose of making peace.

Finally, Jesus said that believers, who experience the resurrection of the righteous dead, are also called the "sons of God."

Consequently, the terms "son of God" and "sons of God" are used of others in Scripture apart from Jesus Christ.

QUESTION 14

If Others Are Called "The Son Of God" In Scripture In What Sense Is Jesus Different?

Jesus Christ is called the "Son of God." This title was acknowledged before His birth by the angel Gabriel. God the Father also publically acknowledged Jesus as His "beloved Son."

However, we also find in Scripture human beings, as well as created heavenly beings, being called "sons of God." Indeed, Adam is called the "son of God" in Luke's genealogy. The nation Israel, in the Old Testament, is called God's son. Heavenly beings, in the Book of Job, are also given this title.

In fact, Jesus said those who are the peacemakers shall be called the "sons of God." Finally, Jesus also taught that those who believed in Him will be called the "sons of God."

If human beings, and created heavenly beings, can be called, "sons of God," then, in what sense, if any, is Jesus different? What makes Him so special?

JESUS POSSESSES THE SAME NATURE AS GOD

The answer is that Jesus was the unique "Son of God" in that He possesses the same nature as God. Adam was the "son of God" in the sense that He was created directly by God. Indeed, he did not have a human father or mother.

The created heavenly beings are the "sons of God" in the sense that they were directly created by God. Israel was symbolically called God's son, as were the peacemakers. Believers are "sons of God" or "children of God" by placing their faith in Christ.

Therefore, the sonship attributed to them is different than the sonship which is attributed to Jesus.

HUMANS BECOME CHILDREN OF GOD

John wrote about how people become "sons of God." It is by believing in Jesus. He said.

> But as many as received Him, to them He gave the right to become children of God, to those who believe in His name (John 1:12 NKJV).

Thus, humans can become "sons of God" or "children of God" in the sense of being part of God's family. This occurs when a person places their faith in Christ.

Jesus, however, is "the" Son of God. He is different from all others for the following reasons.

1. JESUS HAS BEEN GOD'S SON FOR ALL ETERNITY

First, we find that Jesus has been God the Son for all eternity. The Bible explains Jesus' relationship with God the Father in the first chapter of John. It reads.

> No one has ever seen God, but God the One and Only, who is at the Father's side, has made him known (John 1:18 NIV).

Jesus is called "God the One and Only." He has always existed as God. Indeed, there was never a time when He came into existence. This, of course, is not true with respect to humans and created heavenly beings. They came into existence at a certain point in time.

While Jesus, God the Son, has been God for all eternity, He came to earth two thousand years ago. In doing so, He became an actual human being.

In Luke's gospel, we read the words of the angel Gabriel as he addressed Mary. He announced that she would conceive a Son, Jesus. In explaining the nature of that Son, we find that He will be both human and divine. We read the following explanation in Luke.

> He will be a great man and will be called the Son of the Most High. The Lord God will give him the throne of his ancestor David. Your son will be king of Jacob's people forever, and his kingdom will never end." Mary asked the angel, "How can this be? I've never had sexual intercourse." The angel answered her, "The Holy Spirit will come to you, and the power of the Most High will overshadow you. Therefore, the holy child developing inside you will be called the Son of God (Luke 1:32-35 God's Word).

Notice that the angel Gabriel says that the child will develop in the womb. He will be human. However, He will also have the title "Son of God" because He is God who will become a human being.

2. JESUS IS NOT THE NOT LITERAL OFFSPRING OF GOD

Hence, the title "Son of God" does not indicate Jesus was the literal offspring of His Father. As we just mentioned, the Bible speaks of God the Son as having existed as God from all eternity. John also wrote.

> In the beginning was the word, and the word was with God, and the word was God (John 1:1 KJV).

He did not have a beginning as you or I have had. Therefore, He is not a "son" in the sense of a literal offspring. He existed before He was born as a babe in Bethlehem.

3. THE WORD SON CAN MEAN "POSSESSING THE NATURE OF"

Why then do we find the word "Son" used of Jesus? Doesn't this have the idea of a literal offspring? Not always. The Bible often uses the word "son" to mean, "possessing the nature of," or, "on the order of." For example, we read in Paul's letter to the Ephesians.

> And you He made alive, who were dead in trespasses and sins, in which you once walked according to the course of this world, according to the prince of the power of the air, the spirit who now works in the sons of disobedience (Ephesians 2:1,2 NKJV).

The "sons of disobedience" are those who, by nature, are disobedient. Indeed, they are not a literal offspring of disobedience!

In the Old Testament, we read of the "sons of the prophets." The Bible says.

> One of the sons of the prophets said to his fellow prophet by the word of the LORD, "Strike me!" But the man refused to strike him (1 Kings 20:35 HCSB).

These were not the literal offspring of the prophets but rather those who were of the same order as the prophets.

In addition, the sons of the prophets were not inferior to the prophets but were rather equal to them. Therefore, we find that this word translated as "sons" can mean someone other than a literal offspring of another person, but, as in this illustration, having the same authority as that person.

4. JESUS HAS THE SAME NATURE AS GOD

As we discovered, the word translated "son" in Scripture can mean "possessing the nature of." In the same way, we find that Jesus possesses the same nature as the God of the Bible. The Scripture has the following to say about His identity.

For in Christ the fullness of God lives in a human body (Colossians 2:9 NLT).

Jesus Christ possesses the same nature as God—because He is God.

In his first letter, the Apostle John wrote that Jesus Christ, the Son of God, is the true God. He put it this way.

And we know that the Son of God has come and has given us insight to know him who is true, and we are in him who is true, in his Son Jesus Christ. This one is the true God and eternal life (1 John 5:20 NET).

Therefore, He is the Son in the sense that He possesses the same nature as God, or is of the same order of being as God.

THIS IS IN LINE WITH THE OLD TESTAMENT

Thanks to recent discoveries, we now know that this term "Son of God" has its background rooted in the Old Testament. Scholar Craig Evans explains.

At one time it was fashionable to assert that the early confession of Messiah Jesus as 'Son of God' arose not from Jewish and Old Testament antecedents (2 Sam. 7.14; Ps. 2.2,7, for example) but from the influence of the Greco-Roman world, where Greek kings and Roman emperors were hailed as sons of the gods. The discovery of 4Q246 [from the Dead Sea Scrolls] comprising two columns of Aramaic text from Qumran's fourth cave, demolished this view. The author of this first-century BCE text anticipated the coming of a deliverer who will be called 'Son of God' and 'Son of the Most High.' The remarkable parallels to the language of the annunciation (Luke 1.31-35) are widely acknowledged. It seems that the Aramaic-speaking Jews at least one generation before the time of Jesus hoped for a messiah who would be described in rather exalted terms. Post-Easter competition with the Roman imperial cult was not required for the followers of Jesus to speak of their risen Master as the Son of God (Craig Evans, *Jesus and His World: The Archaeological Evidence*, Westminster, John Knox Press, Louisville, Kentucky, 2012, p. 3).

Hence, Jesus, as the Son of God in this unique sense, has its background solidly established in the Old Testament.

SUMMARY TO QUESTION 14
IF OTHERS ARE CALLED "THE SON OF GOD" IN SCRIPTURE IN WHAT SENSE IS JESUS DIFFERENT?

Jesus Christ is called the Son of God" in Scripture. Indeed, God the Father, the angel Gabriel, His own disciples, the Apostle Paul, and even the demons acknowledge Him with this title. However, the term "son of God" is also used of Adam, created heavenly beings, the nation Israel, peacemakers, and Christians.

Consequently, in what sense is Jesus different from them?

The answer is found in the way the Bible uses the term "son." We find that it often uses this word "son" in the sense of "possessing the nature of." Jesus is the "Son" of God in this sense. He possesses the same nature of God.

Therefore, the title "Son" does not, in any way, suggest the Son is inferior to the Father, or that He is the literal offspring of God the Father. Indeed, it is not used of Jesus in the way we use the term "son." In fact, the Bible emphasizes that Jesus has been God for all eternity.

When the word "son" is used of humans and created heavenly beings, it is in a different sense. Adam was the direct creation of God. In this sense he was His "son." Israel was God's child in the sense that the Lord birthed the nation to be His unique people in this world.

Created heavenly beings are "sons of God" in the sense that they are God's creation—they were created to serve and worship Him. New Testament believers are "sons of God" because we become part of His family through faith in Christ.

Therefore, in each of these instances, a "son of God" is used a different sense than of Jesus. He is "the" unique Son of God.

Consequently, we should not confuse this special title which belongs to Him alone with a similar designation which speaks of created heavenly beings and humans.

Was Jesus Always The Son Of God?
(The Eternal Generation Of The Son)

There is a question as to whether Jesus was always the eternal Son of God or that He became the Son of God at the time when He came to earth. This is technically called the "eternal generation of the Son."

The Bible says that God the Father had all things handed over to Jesus— God the Son. Jesus Himself said.

> All things have been handed over to me by my Father; and no one knows the Son except the Father, and no one knows the Father except the Son and anyone to whom the Son chooses to reveal him (Matthew 11:27 NRSV).

Does this imply that Jesus had always been in a subordinate role to the Father as God the Son? Or does it mean that at a certain time Jesus willingly became subordinate to God the Father? What does the Bible say? Two issues are involved in this question.

1. The relationship between the nature of the Father and the Son.

2. The relationship between the ways they carry out their respective roles as members of the Trinity.

OPTION 1: DID JESUS BECOME THE SON AT SOME TIME IN THE PAST?

Some Bible teachers believe that Jesus became the Son of God at a certain time in history. There is an Old Testament passage that seems to teach that Jesus did indeed become the Son at some point in time. The psalmist wrote.

> I will declare the decree: The LORD has said to Me, 'You are My Son, Today I have begotten You' (Psalm 2:7 NKJV).

The Lord said to the Son, "Today" I have begotten you. To many, this indicates that He was not the Son until this particular day, or time, when He was "begotten" of the Father. If this is true, then when did it occur? When did the Second Person of the Trinity, become "the Son?"

There are five particular times that are suggested. They include His coming into the world, His baptism, His resurrection, His ascension, or before He came to earth. The arguments for each can basically be summed up as follows.

1. DID HE BECOME THE SON AT HIS BIRTH?

It is argued that Jesus became the Son of God when He became a human being. At the announcement of His birth the angel said to Mary.

> The angel said to her, "The Holy Spirit will come upon you, and the power of the Most High will overshadow you; therefore the child to be born will be holy; he will be called Son of God" (Luke 1:35 NRSV).

Previously to this, Jesus was not the "Son" of God. It was not until His conception as a human being that He took a subordinate role to God the Father.

2. DID JESUS BECOME THE SON AT HIS BAPTISM?

Another view has Jesus becoming God's Son at His baptism. When He was baptized, God the Father announced.

> And there came a voice from heaven: This is My beloved Son. I take delight in Him (Matthew 3:17 HCSB).

When Jesus Christ was about to begin His public ministry, He became the Son—in the sense of being subordinate to the Father at this particular time.

3. WAS IT AT HIS RESURRECTION THAT JESUS BECAME THE SON?

It is also held that Jesus became the Son of God at His resurrection from the dead. Paul wrote the following to the church at Rome.

> Paul, a slave of Christ Jesus, called as an apostle and singled out for God's good news—which He promised long ago through His prophets in the Holy Scriptures—concerning His Son, Jesus Christ our Lord, who was a descendant of David according to the flesh and was established as the powerful Son of God by the resurrection from the dead according to the Spirit of holiness (Romans 1:1-4 HCSB).

Paul's statement is understood to declare that Jesus became God's Son at His resurrection. Previously He had not been.

4. DID JESUS BECOME THE SON AT HIS ASCENSION?

A fourth view has Jesus becoming the Son of God at His ascension. The writer to the Hebrews says.

> The Son is the radiance of God's glory and the exact representation of his being, sustaining all things by his powerful word. After he had provided purification for sins, he sat down at the right hand of the Majesty in heaven. So he became as much superior to the angels as the name he has inherited is superior to theirs (Hebrews 1:3,4 NIV).

Only when He ascended into heaven, and sat down at the right hand, or place of authority, of God the Father did He then become the Son.

5. DID JESUS BECOME THE SON BEFORE HE CAME TO EARTH

A fifth view has Jesus as the Son of God before He came to earth. At some point in time in the distant past, He became the Son. While He was always the eternal God He became "the Son" sometime before His appearance on the earth.

This is a brief summation of the various views as to when Jesus became the "Son." Again, we stress that the issue at hand is when did God the Son become subordinate to God the Father. This question has nothing to do with their nature. Indeed, the Son has always been God.

OPTION 2: JESUS HAS ALWAYS BEEN THE ETERNAL SON OF GOD

While it is possible that Jesus became the Son at some point in time, the best evidence from Scripture seems to be that Jesus has always been the Son of God. The Bible is clear that God is an unchanging God. Indeed, He has always existed as a Trinity—as God the Father, God the Son, and God the Holy Spirit. Consequently, Jesus has always been the Second Person of the Trinity, God the Son.

A. HE HAS ALWAYS BEEN SUBORDINATE TO THE FATHER

Therefore, God the Son has always been in a subordinate role to God the Father. However, this subordinate role says nothing about His character. Indeed, the Bible stresses the fact that He is equal to the Father in His substance or His nature. Indeed, God the Son is fully God.

We may wonder in what sense is the Son subordinate. A possible example of His subordinate role may be found in the creation of the universe. God the Father spoke the words that brought the universe into existence, while God the Son was the agent who brought them to pass. The Bible says of Jesus.

> All things were made through him, and without him was not any thing made that was made (John 1:3 ESV).

Jesus is the One who brought all things into being as the agent of God the Father. Again, He is equal in His character or nature—but subordinate in position or His mission.

B. THIS IS NOT THE SAME AS SUBORDINATIONISM

Saying that God the Son was eternally subordinate to God the Father is not the same as the ancient heresy known as "subordinationism." This false doctrine says the Son was an inferior being to the Father.

Indeed, while it taught that Jesus was the eternal uncreated Son, He was still not equal to the Father in His being or attributes. The early church father Origen held to a form of subordinationism. When the doctrine of the Trinity was clearly formulated at the council of Nicea, then this heresy, along with others, was rejected.

JESUS IS EQUAL BUT SUBORDINATE

Therefore, the biblical position is that God the Son is equal in His being or character to God the Father, however, He is subordinate in His role. We know that when Jesus Christ returns He will give all things back to God the Father and submit Himself to the Him. Paul wrote the following to the Corinthians.

> And when everything is subject to Him, then the Son Himself will also be subject to Him who subjected everything to Him, so that God may be all in all (1 Corinthians 15:28 HCSB).

This seems to be a further example of God the Son taking a position of subordination to God the Father.

In sum, while there are those who believe that Jesus Christ became the Son of God at some point in time, it seems more consistent with the teaching of Scripture that He has always been God the Son in a subordinate role to God the Father.

SUMMARY TO QUESTION 15
WAS JESUS ALWAYS THE SON OF GOD? (THE ETERNAL GENERATION OF THE SON)

There has been a debate in the church as to whether Jesus Christ was the eternal Son of God, or that He became the Son of God at some point in time. The issue is not His nature or character. Indeed, everyone who believes the Bible understands that God the Son, Jesus, always has been the eternal God. This is not at issue. The question is when did He assume a submissive role with God the Father?

There are those who advocate that Jesus became the Son of God at some specific point in time. Yet, they do not all agree as exactly when this happened. Arguments have been made for His birth, baptism, resurrection and ascension. Some argue that it was sometime before He came to earth.

While there is no agreement as to when He became the Son, it is agreed that this was not His eternal relationship with God the Father. The Son placed Himself in a submissive role to God to the Father at some specific point in time.

Scriptures, however, seem to teach that God the Son has always been in a subordinate role to God the Father while still being equal in character. While God the Son, Jesus, has always been the eternal God, it appears that He has forever been in this subordinate position. We again stress that subordination does not mean inferiority.

This is not to be confused with the ancient heresy of subordinationism. This doctrine taught that Jesus was the eternal God but that He was inferior in His attributes to God the Father. This is why He was in a subordinate position to the Father. This false doctrine was quickly dispensed with when the exact relationship between the Father and Son was more clearly understood.

Therefore, we can conclude that the best position to take on this issue is one which assumes that the Son, while equal to the Father in all of His attributes, has assumed a position of subordination within the Trinity. However, we must be careful not to draw too many conclusions on this matter because there are so many things about God and His workings, which have not been revealed to us.

In What Sense Was Jesus Christ God
And Man Simultaneously?
(The Hypostatic Union)

The Bible teaches that Jesus Christ was the eternal God who became a human being. Indeed, He did not possess a human nature until His birth in the little town of Bethlehem. This doctrine that Jesus Christ was both God and man simultaneously is known as the "hypostatic union." "Hypostatic" is derived from two Greek words, *huper* which means, "under," and *histayme* which means, "to stand."

THE HYPOSTATIC UNION DEFINED

The hypostatic union can be defined as God the Son, the Second Person of the Trinity, came to earth and took human nature upon Himself. Therefore, Jesus of Nazareth was fully God and fully human. He will remain this way forever.

Consequently, when God the Son came to earth, He took upon Himself an additional nature—one that is human. The result was that Jesus Christ was God and humanity simultaneously. Jesus, therefore, was the "God- Man."

JESUS WAS THE GOD-MAN (THEANTHROPIC MAN)

One phrase that is often used to describe Jesus is that He is a "theanthropic man." Theanthropic comes from two Greek words, *theos*, which means God and *anthropos* which means "man" or "human being."

THIS IS A DIFFICULT DOCTRINE

The hypostatic union is a difficult doctrine to comprehend. There are many questions that arise concerning Jesus' divine nature and His human nature.

How are we to understand His two natures in the one body? Did each of them work separately? Were they independent of one another? A number of observations need to be made as we attempt to answer these and other related questions.

1. GOD BECAME A HUMAN BEING IN THE PERSON OF JESUS CHRIST

The first point which we need to stress is that the Bible says that God the Son came to earth. He became a human being John wrote.

> This is how you can recognize the Spirit of God: Every spirit that acknowledges that Jesus Christ has come in the flesh is from God (1 John 4:2 NIV).

The phrase "has come in the flesh" means that Jesus was a human being. Those who confess to this truth belong to God. Those who deny it do not.

John also wrote the following about how God became a human being in the Person of Jesus Christ.

> So the Word became human and lived here on earth among us. He was full of unfailing love and faithfulness. And we have seen his glory, the glory of the only Son of the Father (John 1:14 NLT).

These passages tell us that God the Son came to earth in a "human nature." Therefore, human nature became an element in His one personality and overall makeup.

2. THE BIBLE TEACHES THE UNITY OF JESUS' TWO NATURES

God the Son, Jesus Christ became a human being at a certain point in time. While He was both God and human at the same time, He was only "one" Person.

Consequently, the attributes of Jesus Christ, as well as His titles, are ascribed to the one Person. This can only be understood if He is understood as one single Person who is united with both the human and the divine nature.

We find that both natures are highlighted in the New Testament. Paul wrote about Jesus' human nature as a descendant of King David in the opening chapter in his letter to the Romans. He said.

> Concerning His Son, Jesus Christ our Lord, who was a descendant of David according to the flesh (Romans 1:3 HCSB).

This statement emphasizes Jesus' humanity. Jesus was in the family line of His ancestor David.

Simon Peter wrote of Jesus' human body that suffered and died. He put it this way in his first letter to the believers.

> Christ also suffered when he died for our sins once for all time. He never sinned, but he died for sinners that he might bring us safely home to God. He suffered physical death, but he was raised to life in the Spirit (1 Peter 3:18 NLT).

Physical death gives further evidence to Jesus' humanity. Indeed, to die He had to be a genuine human.

However, the deity of Jesus Christ is also stressed. Indeed, the writer to the Hebrews stated that the Son, Jesus, is the exact representation of God. He said.

But now in these final days, he has spoken to us through his Son. God promised everything to the Son as an inheritance, and through the Son he made the universe and everything in it. The Son reflects God's own glory, and everything about him represents God exactly. He sustains the universe by the mighty power of his command. After he died to cleanse us from the stain of sin, he sat down in the place of honor at the right hand of the majestic God of heaven (Hebrews 1:2,3 NLT).

Jesus is the exact representation of God in every area. This includes His divine nature.

3. JESUS IS ONE PERSON WITH TWO NATURES

It is important that we realize that God the Son had no human personality, or human nature, before He was born as a babe in Bethlehem. Indeed, He only had a divine nature. However, once He became a human being, His human nature was never separate from the divine nature.

Therefore, Jesus, God the Son, was one Person with two natures. He did not cease being God when He became a human—neither was He any less human because He was God. In one body, He was God and humanity united. Jesus was, therefore, the God-man. Consequently, He remained God when He became a human.

4. THE TWO NATURES ARE COMPLETE

The union of the two natures was complete. This means that Jesus did not act as God on some occasions, and then as a human at other times. He was acting as both God and human at the same time.

Therefore, we cannot divide events in His life into the category of human or divine. He lived and suffered as a human being, yet all the while He was God.

Hence, it is not correct to say that He performed miracles as God but died on the cross as a human. Jesus was both divine and human at all times. He is a single, undivided person. That is, the two natures are inseparably united. Thus, He is not merely God and man but rather the "God-man."

5. JESUS WAS A SINGULAR PERSON

We should also note that Jesus spoke of Himself as a single Person. There is no conversation back and forth between the human and divine nature as we find the members of the Trinity addressing each other. For example, in His prayer to the Father, Jesus said.

> I in them, and You in Me; that they may be made perfect in one, and that the world may know that You have sent Me, and have loved them as You have loved Me (John 17:23 NKJV).

Jesus never spoke of Himself in the plural, us. The only possible exception to this is found in John's gospel.

> Most assuredly, I say to you, We speak what We know and testify what We have seen, and you do not receive Our witness (John 3:11 NKJV).

However, this is not necessarily Jesus speaking. It could be John's commentary. If it was Jesus speaking, then He was probably referring to John the Baptist.

The fact that the Messiah was both human and divine is something which the Old Testament anticipated. Indeed, the prophet Isaiah predicted this. He wrote the following.

> For to us a child is born, to us a son is given, and the government will be on his shoulders. And he will be called Wonderful Counselor, Mighty God, Everlasting Father, Prince of Peace (Isaiah 9:6 NIV).

This testifies to both His humanity and His deity. The child which is born will be called "Mighty God."

6. THE TWO NATURES ARE NECESSARY TO SAVE HUMANITY

There is something else which is important for us to understand. The two natures of Jesus Christ are necessary for the salvation of the human race. As a human being, Jesus could represent humanity and die as a human being. As God, His death would have infinite value. Indeed, Peter wrote about the value of the death of Christ.

> For you know that you were redeemed from your empty way of life inherited from the fathers, not with perishable things, like silver or gold, but with the precious blood of Christ, like that of a lamb without defect or blemish (1 Peter 1:18,19 HCSB).

It is impossible to put a price on the death of Jesus. Nothing in the entire universe was as valuable as the life of the Son of God.

7. THE TWO NATURES ARE NECESSARY FOR JESUS TO BE A HIGH PRIEST

We also find that the union of the two natures into one Person is essential for Jesus to be the intermediary, or go-between, between God and humanity. Paul wrote to Timothy about this important truth.

> For there is one God and one intermediary between God and humanity, Christ Jesus, himself human (1 Timothy 2:5 NET).

The only way by which a person can reach the one God is through the intermediary which God has provided, Jesus Christ.

His dual nature is what allows Him to be involved with both God and humanity. The writer to the Hebrews put it this way.

> Therefore, it was necessary for Jesus to be in every respect like us, his brothers and sisters, so that he could be our merciful and

faithful High Priest before God. He then could offer a sacrifice that would take away the sins of the people. Since he himself has gone through suffering and temptation, he is able to help us when we are being tempted (Hebrews 2:17,18 NLT).

God the Son has suffered the limitations of being a human being. This allows Him to have the position as our Great High Priest. He is the One who offers our prayers to God the Father.

The writer to the Hebrews emphasized that Jesus Christ, our High Priest, understands our weaknesses and temptations. He wrote the following words.

> This High Priest of ours understands our weaknesses, for he faced all of the same temptations we do, yet he did not sin. So let us come boldly to the throne of our gracious God. There we will receive his mercy, and we will find grace to help us when we need it (Hebrews 4:15,16 NLT).

Therefore, the God-man, Jesus Christ, intercedes on behalf of humans to God the Father.

In sum, we discover that the doctrine of the hypostatic union is something that is important for us to understand—if we want to truly appreciate Jesus Christ and the mission that He was sent to accomplish.

SUMMARY TO QUESTION 16
IN WHAT SENSE WAS JESUS CHRIST GOD AND MAN SIMULTANEOUSLY? (THE HYPOSTATIC UNION)

The biblical account of Jesus' life demonstrates that Jesus Christ was God and man simultaneously. Indeed, while He was God from all eternity, at a certain time in our past history, God the Son became a human being in the Person of Jesus Christ. Among other things, this is known as the "hypostatic union." It is vital that we understand certain things about this all-important doctrine.

Until the time God the Son became a human being, He had only one nature—a divine nature. Yet at a particular time in our history, He took upon Himself another nature—a human nature.

It is essential to realize that Jesus Christ was fully God and fully human at the same time. He was not half-God, half-human. These two natures in God the Son, which resided in one body, cannot be divided.

In other words, He did not do some things as God, and other things as a human. Everything He did was as the God-man. Thus, it is not possible to divide His actions into categories of human or divine.

The Bible also says that His human-divine nature is necessary for our salvation from sin. Indeed, Jesus had to be a human to die for other humans. Yet His humanity had to be perfect to be an acceptable sacrifice to God.

Furthermore, as God, we also discover that His death had infinite worth. Nothing in the entire universe was as valuable as His life.

Therefore, we find that His two natures are necessary for Jesus to be our Great High Priest. Since He has lived on the earth as a human being, He certainly understands what we humans suffer. Consequently, He can identify with us and our limitations and sufferings. As God, He can speak directly to God the Father on our behalf.

Therefore, in looking at what the Scripture has to say about Jesus' two natures, we find that it is an extremely important doctrine. Indeed, it is something which all believers should take the time to seriously study.

What Are Some Common Misconceptions About The Two Natures Of Christ?

Jesus Christ had two natures. While He was fully God, He was also completely human. This dual nature of God the Son is sometimes called the "hypostatic union." It is an important New Testament doctrine.

Unfortunately, there are a number of misconceptions about Christ's dual nature, or the hypostatic union, that need to be cleared up. They are as follows.

MISCONCEPTION 1: GOD DID NOT TURN INTO A HUMAN BEING

The Bible does not teach that God turned into a human in the Person of Jesus Christ. God the Son, Jesus, remained God during His entire time on the earth—as well as He does today.

Actually it would be impossible for God to cease being God. God, by definition, is eternal and unchanging. He had no beginning and will have no end. It is impossible for Him to cease to exist. In addition, His attributes cannot change—He cannot stop being the unchangeable God.

MISCONCEPTION 2: JESUS IS NOT MERELY A MAN OF GOD

The hypostatic union does not mean that Jesus Christ was merely a man of God. While He was a man of God in the ultimate sense of the term, He was certainly much more than that. He was the God-Man—God in human flesh. Consequently, it is not correct to put Him into the category of a godly man.

MISCONCEPTION 3: GOD DID NOT LIVE IN A BODY

The hypostatic union does not mean that God the Son simply lived in a human body. Indeed, Jesus Christ was thoroughly human who suffered all of the limitations of a human body. The Bible stresses that Jesus had a human nature, as well as a divine nature. He was God and human at the same time.

MISCONCEPTION 4: THEY HYPOSTATIC UNION IS NOT THE SAME AS THE VIRGIN BIRTH

Often the hypostatic union is confused with the virgin birth. The virgin birth, or virgin conception, speaks of the manner in which Jesus came into the world. The hypostatic union refers to the fact that Jesus Christ was fully God and fully human. It is a result of the virgin birth but not the same thing as the virgin birth. This distinction must be kept in mind.

MISCONCEPTION 5: IT IS NOT THE SAME AS THE INCARNATION

The hypostatic union is not the same as the incarnation. The incarnation refers to the entire story of God the Son becoming a human being. The hypostatic union is merely one part of the story of Jesus becoming human—it is not the entire story.

MISCONCEPTION 6: IT WAS NOT A THEOPHANY (A TEMPORARY APPEARANCE OF GOD)

The hypostatic union is not a theophany. A theophany is the temporary appearance of God in a human body. There were a number of occasions of this occurring—which the Old Testament records. What the hypostatic union and theophanies have in common is the idea that God took on a human body. However, the hypostatic union occurred only once, whereas there have been several theophanies recorded in Scripture.

In addition, the theophanies were *temporary* appearances of God in a body. Each one lasted for only a short period of time. God the Son came to earth in a human body that lasted approximately thirty years. Furthermore, the union of the two natures in Jesus Christ is permanent.

This sums up some of the common misconceptions we find about the two natures of Jesus Christ. It is important that we have a proper understanding of who He is—as well as who He is not.

SUMMARY TO QUESTION 17:
WHAT ARE SOME COMMON MISCONCEPTIONS ABOUT THE TWO NATURES OF JESUS CHRIST?

The Bible teaches that God became a human being in the Person of Jesus Christ. God the Son, the Second Person of the Holy Trinity, left the glory of heaven to live among us. This is the central teaching of the New Testament. It is known as the "hypostatic union."

There are, however, a number of misconceptions about the hypostatic union that need to be addressed. We can cite them as follows.

The union of the two natures of Christ does not mean that God turned into a human being. God the Son added something which He did not previously possess—a human body. However, God did not turn into a human!

Neither does it mean that Jesus Christ, God the Son, was merely a man of God. He was indeed the godliest man who has ever existed but He is much more than this. Jesus is the eternal God who came to this earth.

The idea of the union of Christ's two natures does not mean that God merely took on a human body, or lived in a human body. Jesus was one hundred percent human, as well as one hundred percent divine. God was not merely living in a body.

Neither was the hypostatic union the same thing as the incarnation. The term incarnation refers to the entire story of God becoming human. The hypostatic union is merely one aspect of it.

Finally, the hypostatic union is not the same as a theophany—a temporary appearance of God in a body. While the Old Testament records that God took upon Himself a human body on several occasions, there is a big difference between these appearances and what occurred with Jesus.

Each of the theophanies was for a short period of time. God the Son lived for over thirty years on the earth in a human body. In other words, it was not temporary.

In addition, once God the Son took on this human body the two natures have become permanent.

This sums up some of the common misconceptions we find about the hypostatic union—that God the Son became a human being in the Person of Jesus Christ. Since this is an important New Testament doctrine, it is important that these misconceptions be cleared up.

QUESTION 18

How Could Christ Be God And Human At The Same Time? (The Communion Of Attributes)

Jesus Christ was fully God and fully human. The attributes of both natures of the God-man were expressed in the one Person. This means that there was no mixing of the natures, or any division of His Person. He was one united Person with both human and divine attributes. This is known as the "communion of attributes." The fact that Christ had attributes of both of God and humanity is clearly taught in Scripture.

SOME PRELIMINARY OBSERVATIONS NEED TO BE MADE ABOUT THIS ISSUE

Before we attempt to answer this question, there are a number of preliminary points which need to be made—as we seek to find answers to these issues about the dual natures of Christ.

OBSERVATION 1: JESUS' CHRIST WAS IN A UNIQUE SITUATION

The fact that Jesus had both a perfect human nature, as well as a divine nature, is something that is unique in history. Therefore, we have nothing anywhere with which to compare it. We must always remember this when we attempt to give answers to questions concerning how the two natures worked with each other.

Therefore, we cannot, and we should not, attempt to answer these questions by comparing it to things we do know and understand. Indeed, there are no real points of comparison.

OBSERVATION 2: THERE IS A MYSTERY ABOUT GOD BECOMING A HUMAN

This brings us to our next point. The Apostle Paul wrote of the mystery of God becoming a human being in the Person of Jesus Christ. He wrote the following to Timothy.

> Beyond all question, the mystery of godliness is great: He appeared in a body, was vindicated by the Spirit, was seen by angels, was preached among the nations, was believed on in the world, was taken up in glory (1 Timothy 3:16 NIV).

There is an element that is certainly beyond our understanding as we consider the issues around Jesus' human nature and His divine nature.

Paul wrote to the Colossians about this plan of God which was unknown to previous generations. That is the plan that God would become a human being. The apostle wrote.

> My goal is that they will be encouraged and knit together by strong ties of love. I want them to have full confidence because they have complete understanding of God's secret plan, which is Christ himself (Colossians 2:2 NLT).

The hypostatic union, that Jesus was both fully human and fully divine at the same time, is ultimately a mystery. We cannot understand it any more than we can understand the doctrine of the Trinity. While it is a mystery, it is certainly not irrational. We believe in the hypostatic union is a reality because it is taught in Scripture by a God who is unable to deceive.

WHAT THE SCRIPTURES TEACH ABOUT JESUS' TWO NATURES

Now that we have looked at some preliminary matters, the following points need to be made about His humanity as well as His deity.

1. JESUS IS CALLED GOD, YET HE WAS HUMAN

To begin with, Jesus is God the Son. John's gospel begins as follows.

In the beginning was the word, and the word was with God, and the word was God (John 1:1 KJV).

The Word, Jesus, was in the beginning with God.

Though Jesus was called God, He was also recognized as a genuine human being. For example, the centurion at Jesus' crucifixion testified to His humanity.

And when the centurion, who stood there in front of Jesus, saw how he died, he said, "Surely this man was the Son of God" (Mark 15:39 NIV).

He realized Jesus was a man. Yet He was much more than a man. Indeed, Jesus was both human and divine.

2. JESUS WAS THE FULLNESS OF DEITY, BUT HE HAD A BODY OF FLESH AND BONES

We also find that the fullness of deity dwelt in Him. Paul wrote the following to the Colossians about this essential truth.

For in Christ the fullness of God lives in a human body (Colossians 2:9 NLT).

All of God's fullness dwelt in Jesus.

Yet Jesus had an actual body of flesh and bones. Indeed, Jesus said the following to His frightened disciples on the day of His resurrection when He appeared to them in a locked room.

Look at my hands and my feet and see who I am! Touch me and find out for yourselves. Ghosts don't have flesh and bones as you see I have (Luke 24:39 CEV).

Jesus was a genuine human with a body of flesh and bones. If this were not so, He could not have told the disciples to handle His resurrected body. Yet, He was also fully God.

3. JESUS EXISTED BEFORE ABRAHAM, YET WAS BORN DURING THE REIGN OF AUGUSTUS CAESAR

Jesus Himself made the astounding claim that He existed before the patriarch Abraham—a man who lived some two thousand years before Christ. In John's gospel, we read of what He said to the religious rulers who asked Him about His identity.

> Jesus said to them, "I assure you: Before Abraham was, I am" (John 8:58 HCSB).

Jesus of Nazareth claimed that He was in existence before Abraham. Clearly, He claimed to more than a mere man.

Yet this Person, who claimed to have existed before Abraham, was born in the reign of Caesar Augustus. Luke records the moment His mother Mary gave birth.

> In those days a decree went out from Caesar Augustus that all the world should be registered. . . And while they were there, the time came for her to give birth. And she gave birth to her firstborn son and wrapped him in swaddling cloths and laid him in a manger, because there was no place for them in the inn (Luke 2:1,6,7 ESV).

Again, we have the contrast between the human Jesus and the divine Jesus. The divine Son of God became a baby in a manger in Bethlehem.

4. JESUS KNEW ALL THINGS, YET HE GREW IN WISDOM

The Bible stresses that Jesus knew all things. After His resurrection, in a conversation with Simon Peter, we read the following.

> He [Jesus] asked him the third time, "Simon, son of John, do you love Me?" Peter was grieved that He asked him the third time, "Do you love Me?" He said, "Lord, You know everything! You know that I love You." "Feed My sheep," Jesus said (John 21:17 HCSB).

Peter acknowledged that the Lord knew "all things."

However, in the Gospel of Luke, we read that the human Jesus actually grew in wisdom. The Bible says.

> And Jesus increased in wisdom and stature, and in favor with God and with people (Luke 2:52 HCSB).

The contrast is striking—Jesus knew all things yet grew in wisdom.

5. JESUS WAS WITHOUT SIN, YET HE WAS TEMPTED

Jesus Christ, God the Son, was without sin. The writer to the Hebrews stated this about as clear as it can be stated.

> We have a chief priest who is able to sympathize with our weaknesses. He was tempted in every way that we are, but he didn't sin (Hebrews 4:15 God's Word).

Jesus did not sin!

Yet Mathew wrote about Jesus' temptation to sin. Indeed, after He was baptized in the Jordan River, we read the following took place.

> Then was Jesus led up of the Spirit into the wilderness to be tempted of the devil (Matthew 4:1 KJV).

Jesus, the One who was without sin, was tempted to sin. Yet, as the Bible tells us, He refused to submit to sin.

6. JESUS RECEIVED PRAYER, YET HE PRAYED TO THE FATHER

We find that Jesus was addressed in prayer. In the Book of Acts, we find that the martyr Stephen prayed directly to Jesus as he was dying. It says.

> And as they stoned him, Stephen prayed, "Lord Jesus, receive my spirit" (Acts 7:59 NLT).

Stephen recognized that he could pray directly to Jesus. It did not trouble him to address Jesus Himself in prayer.

Yet Jesus Christ prayed to His Father during His time here upon the earth. Indeed, on the night of His betrayal we read the following words which He said.

> Jesus spoke these things, looked up to heaven, and said: Father, the hour has come. Glorify Your Son so that the Son may glorify You (John 17:1 HCSB).

Jesus prayed to God the Father, yet He Himself received prayers as God the Son. Again we find the contrast.

7. JESUS GIVES ETERNAL LIFE, YET HE EXPERIENCED DEATH

The Bible says that it is Jesus alone who grants eternal life. Jesus Himself made this clear. He made the following claim.

> I give them eternal life, and they will never perish. No one will snatch them out of my hand (John 10:28 NRSV).

Jesus is the Giver of eternal life.

Yet, Jesus died. The Bible says.

> Once again Jesus shouted, and then he died (Matthew 27:50 CEV).

One of the great ironies about Jesus' life and ministry is that the One who offers eternal life for those who believe in Him also experienced physical death for these same people. Indeed, He died so that each of us could live.

THERE ARE THREE IMPORTANT TRUTHS NEED TO BE RECOGNIZED

There are three important things which should be emphasized about these facts concerning the two natures of God the Son, Jesus Christ.

They include the following.

JESUS CHRIST HAD TWO DISTINCT NATURES, ONE HUMAN AND ONE DIVINE

First, Jesus Christ had two distinct natures. He was fully God and fully human. The evidence is clear. There is no doubt whatsoever that the New Testament teaches this truth.

THERE WAS NO MINGLING OR MIXING OF THE NATURES

Second, there was no intermingling between the two natures. He has been God for all eternity—but only became human at a point in time. When He became human, God the Son took upon Himself a nature which He did not previously have.

HE WAS ONLY ONE PERSON

Finally, while God the Son, Jesus Christ, had two natures, He was only one Person. He was not a dual personality. Neither did He do some things as God, and other things as a human.

Therefore, while we look at what Scripture has to tell us about the Person of Jesus Christ, and the attributes He possessed as both God and man, we must recognize His uniqueness, as well as the unique nature of this subject. Indeed, there is nobody else to whom we can compare Him.

SUMMARY TO QUESTION 18
HOW COULD CHRIST BE BOTH GOD AND HUMAN AT THE SAME TIME? (THE COMMUNION OF ATTRIBUTES)

The Bible teaches that two thousand years ago God the Son became a human being. Jesus Christ, in one body, was both God and human. The great truth of the New Testament is that the eternal God came to our earth like one of us, fully human. This is known as the "communion of attributes."

Obviously there are so many questions which arise about this essential truth of the Christian faith. It is important that we have answers to these questions.

There are two preliminary truths that must be appreciated.

To begin with, Jesus Christ is unique. Never in our history has God become a human being and lived among us. Therefore, we have absolutely nobody else with which to compare Him. This being the case, we should resist the temptation of attempting to explain Jesus, being both God and human at the same time, with comparisons or analogies which are familiar to us. We should not attempt to do this because there is no real comparison to anything, anywhere. This must be understood.

We also must understand that there is a certain degree of mystery with Jesus being fully God and fully human at the same time. Scripture itself speaks of it this way. Consequently, there should be a number of questions about this topic that we cannot answer.

Again, we must realize our limitations. God has given us sufficient answers to our questions about God the Son becoming a human being— but He certainly has not told us everything. Therefore, we must realize that we will have a number of unanswered questions when we look at this subject.

Having said this, we can now look at the contrasts between His two natures as it is taught in Scripture.

First, the Bible states that Jesus was both God and human at the same time. There is no doubt about this. Jesus was the fullness of deity, God Himself. Yet He had a body of flesh and bones and He suffered all the limitations of humanity. How this could be is not explained for us in the New Testament—it is merely taught.

There is also the contrast in His humanity and deity with respect to His birth. Jesus claimed that He existed before the man Abraham—the patriarch who lived some two thousand years before the time of Christ. Yet the Bible says that Jesus was born during the reign of Caesar Augustus. Again, we see the contrast between His humanity and deity.

The Bible says that God the Son, Jesus, knew all things. Indeed, one of the attributes of God is that He is omniscient—He has all knowledge. Yet we are also told that He grew in wisdom. While these two truths are taught, there is no explanation given as to how each of these things can be true at the same time.

Scripture says that Jesus was without sin His entire life. There is no doubt about this. Yet Scripture tells us that He was tempted to sin. Again, there is no explanation for how this can be.

People prayed directly to Jesus. As God, He can rightly receive our prayers. Yet Jesus Himself prayed to God the Father while He was here upon the earth. This is another example of His humanity and His deity both being evident.

Finally, Jesus is the One who gives eternal life to those who believe in Him. Only He can offer this to humanity. However, Jesus Himself, the Life-giver, experienced physical death on our behalf.

Consequently, the contrast between the two natures of Jesus is highlighted in a number of different ways. While His humanity and deity are taught side-by-side in Scripture, we are never told how this can be.

As we stated in our introduction to this question, there is indeed much mystery regarding the union of God Himself with perfect humanity. Therefore, as we seek to answer some of these questions, we must do so while recognizing our limitations.

In What Sense Did Jesus Empty Himself?
(Kenosis, Condescension Of Christ)

In the second chapter of the letter to the Philippians, the Apostle Paul wrote about Jesus Christ and His coming to the earth. He explained it this way.

> Your attitude should be the same as that of Christ Jesus: Who, being in very nature God, did not consider equality with God something to be grasped, but made himself nothing, taking the very nature of a servant, being made in human likeness. And being found in appearance as a man, he humbled himself and became obedient to death—even death on a cross! (Philippians 2:5-8 NIV).

This passage speaks of Jesus Christ "emptying Himself." The Greek word for this is "kenosis." The question is what did Jesus empty Himself of when He came to earth?

Since there have been many attempts to explain exactly what was meant by this term, it is important that we have a proper understanding of what Paul is teaching.

ANSWER: JESUS EMPTIED HIMSELF IN THREE WAYS

The best answer seems to be that Jesus emptied Himself in at least three different ways. First, He voluntarily accepted the limitations of being a human being. Second, His glory was hidden from the people. Third, He gave up the independent use of His relative attributes as God (all-knowing, all-powerful, everywhere present, etc.).

1. HE EXPERIENCED THE LIMITATIONS OF A HUMAN BEING

It is clear that Jesus is the eternal God. John's gospel begins by explaining the relationship of God the Father to the Word, God the Son.

> In the beginning was the word, and the word was with God, and the word was God (John 1:1 KJV).

The Word, Jesus Christ, not only existed with God in the beginning, He was Himself God!

John also wrote that Jesus, God the Son, became a human being at a particular point in time. He put it this way.

> So the Word became human and lived here on earth among us. He was full of unfailing love and faithfulness. And we have seen his glory, the glory of the only Son of the Father (John 1:14 NLT).

God the Son, Jesus Christ, was still God while He was here upon the earth. However, He took upon Himself an additional nature—that of a human. Jesus had a body like other men—except it was without sin. All the while, He did not set aside any of the attributes that were rightly His.

Yet, He voluntarily limited Himself to being a human being. With genuine humanity came certain restrictions. He could only be at one place at a time. He needed to eat, rest, and sleep. He could feel pain, bleed, and die. Before He became a man, God the Son had no such restrictions.

The self-humbling of God the Son, Jesus Christ, was certainly not against His will. He willingly took on the limitations of humanity. In fact, He never used any of His divine attributes to relieve Himself of the limitations of being a human being. The Bible consistently emphasizes this all-important truth.

2. JESUS' GLORY WAS VEILED

We also find that the glory of Jesus was hidden from humanity during His time on the earth—although it was revealed at certain times. The glory of God was such that no human could look at it and live. This glory that belonged to Jesus was veiled. At the end of His life, Christ prayed to His Father to restore His former glory. We read Him saying.

I have glorified You on the earth by completing the work You gave Me to do. Now, Father, glorify Me in Your presence with that glory I had with You before the world existed (John 17:4,5 HCSB).

After His Ascension, the glory of God the Son was no longer veiled. We read in the Book of Revelation.

When I saw him, I fell at his feet as though dead. But he placed his right hand on me, saying, "Do not be afraid; I am the first and the last" (Revelation 1:17 NRSV).

When John saw Jesus in His glory, He had to fall at His feet as one who was dead.

Jesus had to veil His glory in order to accomplish His mission upon the earth.

3. JESUS DID NOT INDEPENDENTLY USE CERTAIN ATTRIBUTES

There is something else. Jesus chose not to independently exercise some of His attributes. This includes His ability to be all-knowing and all-powerful.

His moral attributes, such as love, holiness, and truth were not set aside in any sense. He did not give His perfect morality but He did give up any independent use of His mighty power.

The key word in this understanding is "independent." On many occasions, we find Christ exercising His attributes of omniscience and omnipotence. Therefore, they were at His disposal to use whenever the situation called for it.

The New Testament stresses the fact that Jesus chose rather to live the life as a servant—One who put His trust in His Heavenly Father. The following statements from Jesus illustrate this truth.

> Very truly I tell you, the Son can do nothing by himself; he can do only what he sees his Father doing, because whatever the Father does the Son also does (John 5:19 NIV).

Jesus said that He only did things that pleased God the Father.

In another place in the Gospel of John, we find Jesus saying that He did the will of the One who sent Him.

> I can do nothing on My own. I judge only as I hear, and My judgment is righteous, because I do not seek My own will, but the will of Him who sent Me (John 5:30 HCSB).

He sought to do the will of God the Father.

Jesus also said that He came from heaven to earth to do the will of God the Father. John also records Him saying this.

> For I have come down from heaven, not to do My own will, but the will of Him who sent Me (John 6:38 NKJV).

We find that Jesus chose to submit to the will of God the Father in every word, and in every deed. Therefore, any independent desire on Jesus' part, to act apart from God the Father, was emptied, or laid aside, while here upon the earth.

Indeed, there are a number of things we find in Scripture to support this idea of Jesus' limitations.

A. JESUS DID NOT KNOW CERTAIN THINGS

The Bible does teach that there were certain things that Jesus did not know. For example, Jesus did not know the time of His Second Coming.

> Now concerning that day or hour no one knows—neither the angels in heaven nor the Son—except the Father (Mark 13:32 HCSB).

At this particular time, Jesus did not know when He would return.

On one occasion, Jesus did not know who it was from the crowd who touched His clothes. Mark records what occurred.

> At once Jesus realized in Himself that power had gone out from Him. He turned around in the crowd and said, "Who touched My robes?" His disciples said to Him, "You see the crowd pressing against You, and You say, 'Who touched Me?' So He was looking around to see who had done this" (Mark 5:30-32 HCSB).

Jesus did not know who touched Him. This further illustrates His limitations as a human being.

When He was here upon the earth, Jesus was all knowing, or omniscient, yet He did not know the time of His Second Coming.

Although He was all-powerful, or omnipotent, He prayed to God to raise Lazarus from the dead.

Jesus, as God, was everywhere present, or omnipresent, but He could only be at one place at a time.

These attributes were always with Him but He simply chose not to use them apart from the will of the Father.

B. JESUS WAS CONTINUOUSLY SELF-LIMITED

The self-limitation of Jesus was something that He continually practiced. This being the case, He had to consciously and continuously rely on the Father instead of His own divine attributes. At the raising of Lazarus, we read the following.

> Then they took away the stone from the place where the dead man was lying. And Jesus lifted up His eyes and said, "Father, I thank You that You have heard Me. And I know that You always hear Me, but because of the people who are standing by I said this, that they may believe that You sent Me" (John 11:41,42 NKJV).

He knew that His Father always heard His prayers, and was constantly with Him. In other words, Jesus was always aware of His Father's presence.

C. HE WAS ALWAYS GUIDED BY THE HOLY SPIRIT

As a human being, Jesus chose to be guided by the Holy Spirit rather than by His own will. Scripture speaks of Jesus being filled, or controlled, with the Spirit after His baptism. We read in Luke.

> And Jesus, full of the Holy Spirit, returned from the Jordan and was led by the Spirit in the wilderness (Luke 4:1 ESV).

Jesus allowed the Spirit of God to lead Him.

Consequently, we find that Jesus performed His miracles by the power of the Holy Spirit. He stated this when He was in a discussion with the religious leaders.

> But if I cast out demons by the Spirit of God, surely the kingdom of God has come upon you (Matthew 12:28 NKJV).

His miraculous works were a result in His trust in God the Father through God the Holy Spirit.

He placed His faith in God the Father. He was able to live a sinless life by trusting the Father at all times. Consequently, believers are told to "walk as He walked" or "live their lives as Christ did." John wrote.

> Whoever says he abides in him ought to walk in the same way in which he walked (1 John 2:6 ESV)

The New Living Translation puts it this way.

> Those who say they live in God should live their lives as Christ did (1 John 2:6 NLT)

This could only be possible if Jesus walked in faith as a human being. Otherwise it would be impossible to live our lives as He lived.

D. JESUS IS ABLE TO UNDERSTAND OUR NEEDS

Jesus willingly limited Himself while here upon the earth. Consequently, He understands what happens to humans. The writer to the Hebrews acknowledged that Jesus realizes our own needs and human limitations. He wrote.

> For we do not have a high priest who is unable to sympathize with our weaknesses, but one who in every respect has been tempted as we are, yet without sin. Let us then with confidence draw near to the throne of grace, that we may receive mercy and find grace to help in time of need (Hebrews 4:15,16 ESV).

He knows our needs, our struggles. Consequently, the Lord can sympathize with us.

In addition, since He has experienced the same problems as humankind, He can comfort us. The Bible says that God is the God of all comfort.

> Praise God, the Father of our Lord Jesus Christ! The Father is a merciful God, who always gives us comfort. He comforts

us when we are in trouble, so that we can share that same comfort with others in trouble (2 Corinthians 1:3,4 CEV).

He comforts us because He knows what we have been experiencing.

Finally, we come to the reason why Jesus imposed these self-limitations upon His Person—He did it because of His love for us.

For God so loved the world, that he gave his only Son, that whoever believes in him should not perish but have eternal life (John 3:16 ESV).

In sum, it was the love of God that caused Jesus to voluntarily humble Himself and lay aside some of the rights that He had as God.

SUMMARY TO QUESTION 19
IN WHAT SENSE DID JESUS EMPTY HIMSELF? (KENOSIS, CONDESCENSION OF CHRIST)

The Bible speaks of God the Son, Jesus Christ, emptying Himself when He came to this earth. This has been called the "kenosis" of Christ after the Greek word which means "emptying." It is also referred to as the condescension of Christ.

While Scripture says that Jesus Christ emptied Himself when He became human, it does not specifically say what He emptied Himself of. While there has been much speculation as to what this consisted of, there are three things which seem to answer the question.

First, God the Son restricted Himself to a human body when He came to earth. He became a fully functioning human being with all its limitations. In doing so, God the Son gave up the position He has enjoyed for all eternity. Indeed, until the time of His coming to the earth, He only had only nature—a divine nature. That divine nature was now joined to a human nature with all the restrictions which come with it.

Second, God the Son veiled, or hid, His glory from the people. Therefore, He emptied Himself of the glory, or majesty, which He has had since before our world was created. In His prayer to God the Father on the night of His betrayal, Jesus asked to have that former glory restored. Consequently, it seems that part of the emptying of Christ concerns the glory He had before becoming a human and coming to the earth.

Finally, Jesus emptied Himself of the right to exercise certain of His divine attributes when He became human. These attributes such as being all-powerful, all-knowing, were exercised by God the Son at certain times in His public ministry. However, it was only done through the will of God the Father.

In other words, it was never on His own initiative. Indeed, His entire life as a human being was lived in obedience to the will of God the Father through the power of God the Holy Spirit. Thus, in this sense, He emptied Himself of any right to independently exercise His own will.

While so much about the Son of God coming to our earth is a mystery, it does seem that these three points help us answer the question as to what He emptied Himself.

We must be careful, however, to believe that we have all the answers to this question—since there is so much about God and His workings which we do not know because it has not been revealed to us. Therefore, it is best that we give tentative answers to this question.

QUESTION 20

What Are Some Common Misconceptions About Jesus Emptying Himself When He Came To The Earth?

The Bible says that Jesus Christ emptied Himself of certain things when He came to this earth. This is also known as the "kenosis" or "emptying of Christ." Much debate has occurred over exactly what He emptied Himself of. The best answer to this question seems to consist of three things.

First, He restricted Himself to live as a human being with all its limitations. In addition, God the Son also laid aside His glory which He has had for all eternity.

Finally, He exercised certain of His divine attributes always in accordance with the will of God the Father, never on His own.

This seems to give us an answer as to what God the Son emptied, or laid aside, when He came to this earth.

WHAT EMPTYING DOES NOT MEAN

This seems to be what the "emptying" of Jesus Christ does mean. However, we should also deal with what the emptying or "kenosis" of Jesus Christ does not mean.

Indeed, there are a number of common misconceptions about what Christ emptied Himself of when He became a human being. These misconceptions need to be cleared up. They include the following.

MISCONCEPTION 1: JESUS SET ASIDE HIS DEITY

This view holds that Jesus ceased to be God when He came to earth. It says He gave up His essential attributes of deity when He became a human. In other words, Jesus was a mere human when He was on the earth and nothing more—He was no longer God.

RESPONSE

Jesus was always conscious of the fact that He was God. Those who say that Jesus ceased being God, when He came to earth, attempt to make Him into a fallible human being with limitations just like the rest of us. If this were the case, then His knowledge of divine mysteries would have been no better than any other human of His day. Consequently, His testimony would carry no real weight. He would not have been competent to speak about any issue with absolute authority.

The Bible does not say that God changed into a human being but rather than God *became* a human being without ceasing to be God. The Bible says that Jesus does not change.

> Jesus Christ the same yesterday, and today, and forever (Hebrews 13:8 KJV).

It is impossible for God's nature to change. His attributes are eternal—they will always remain the same. Therefore, this suggestion cannot answer the question. We must look elsewhere.

MISCONCEPTION 2: JESUS SET ASIDE SOME OF HIS DIVINE ATTRIBUTES

This view contends that Jesus Christ set aside certain of His divine attributes (such as being all-knowing, all-powerful and everywhere-present) when He came to earth. At the same time, He kept some of

His attributes such as holiness, love, and truth, His moral attributes. Therefore, the emptying consisted of divesting Himself of some the characteristics He always possessed as God—but all the while keeping other attributes.

RESPONSE

Jesus Christ is the eternal God. He enjoys all the rights and privileges of that position. If Jesus was God, as the Scripture teaches, it is hard to imagine that He could somehow rid Himself of some of these qualities and still be God. The emptying could not have been with regard to His attributes as God, because, by definition, God cannot cease being God.

MISCONCEPTION 3: JESUS DID NOT KNOW THAT HE WAS GOD

There are some who believe that Jesus did not give up any of His divine attributes while here on earth but rather gave up His divine self-consciousness. In other words, He did not know He was God. All the attributes of deity remained with Him, but He simply was not aware of them. Therefore, He emptied Himself of the knowledge of who He truly is.

RESPONSE

Scripture says that Jesus was completely aware of who He was, and what He could do, at all times. Indeed, when arrested in the Garden of Gethsemane, Jesus stated that He could summon legions of angels who could immediately stop those who were arresting Him. We read.

> Then Jesus told him [Peter], "Put your sword back in place because all who take up a sword will perish by a sword. Or do you think that I cannot call on My Father, and He will provide Me at once with more than 12 legions of angels?" (Matthew 26:52,53 HCSB).

Jesus was indeed aware of whom He was at all times. Nothing in His words or deeds gives the slightest indication that He was ignorant of who He was, or why He was here upon the earth.

MISCONCEPTION 4: JESUS ACTED AS THOUGH HE DID NOT POSSESS DIVINE ATTRIBUTES

This position holds that Jesus still retained all of His divine attributes when He was here on earth but that He acted as though He did not possess them. While He was still all-knowing, all-powerful, and holy, His behavior did not reflect that He still possessed them.

RESPONSE

This answer would mean that Jesus was somehow deceiving the people. He knew who He was, but He pretended to be someone else. This is inconsistent with the pure, holy character of God. It is not possible that God can deceive people about anything. This viewpoint does not fit the facts.

MISCONCEPTION 5: JESUS SET ASIDE THE USE OF HIS DIVINE ATTRIBUTES

This position holds that Jesus gave up the use, not the possession of His divine attributes. While He was fully God during His time here upon the earth, He did not use any of these divine attributes. Though He could have used them, He did not.

RESPONSE

The New Testament teaches that Jesus did exercise the use of His divine attributes while He was here upon the earth. For example, He was able to predict the future accurately.

Indeed, we have a number of predictions made by Jesus concerning coming events. The Bible, as well as secular history, records the fact that Jesus was accurate on each and every one of His predictions. Only God can do something like this. No human being, not even a perfect one, knows what will happen in the future.

This sums up some of the common misconceptions we find with respect to the doctrine of God the Son, Jesus Christ, emptying Himself, when He came to this earth.

SUMMARY TO QUESTION 20:
WHAT ARE SOME COMMON MISCONCEPTIONS ABOUT JESUS EMPTYING HIMSELF WHEN HE CAME TO THE EARTH?

When Jesus came to earth, the Bible says that He laid aside or emptied Himself of something. There are many misconceptions as to what He set aside. Some of the more popular ones include the following.

To begin with, it was not His deity that He set aside. God the Son could not empty Himself of His deity. In other words, He could not stop being God. While He was indeed fully human, He was not merely human—Jesus Christ was God and Man simultaneously.

There is also the misconception that God the Son set aside some of His divine attributes when He became a human being. However, this does not seem possible. As God, it is not possible that He set aside only some of His divine attributes while keeping others.

Some argue that Jesus was God the Son while He was here upon the earth but that He did not know this. In other words, He emptied Himself of the knowledge that He was God. Again, this is the wrong way of looking at what the Bible has to say about Jesus emptying Himself. Jesus always knew He was God and He knew that He possessed these divine attributes. Indeed, He was not ignorant of who He was, or what He could do.

There is also the theory that Jesus, though He had these powers which belong to God alone, acted as though He did not have them. But this viewpoint would make Jesus a deceiver.

Furthermore, we find that Jesus allowed the people to know that He did indeed have such powers which belong to God alone.

Finally, there are those who contend that Jesus set aside the use of certain of His divine attributes while here upon the earth. This includes being all-powerful and all-knowing. However, this does not fit the facts. Those powers were always present with Him and He used them on occasion.

Consequently, when we seek to understand the emptying of Christ, we should reject each of these theories because they do not fit the biblical facts.

Why Did Jesus Call Himself The Son Of Man?

While He was on the earth, Jesus' favorite designation, in referring to Himself, was the "Son of Man." Indeed, the Gospels record some seventy-eight times that Jesus used this title. For example, when He asked His disciples the question about His identity, He put it to them this way.

> When Jesus came to the region of Caesarea Philippi, he asked his disciples, "Who do people say that the Son of Man is?" (Matthew 16:13 NLT).

Though this was the favorite title of Jesus, the New Testament does not define the exact meaning of the title "Son of Man."

What did He mean by this title? Why not call Himself the "Son of God" "the Messiah," or the "Son of David." Each of these titles was rightfully His. Why the emphasis on this particular designation of Himself?

To answer this question, we can make a couple of important observations about the way in which it is used.

1. THE TITLE IS CONNECTED WITH JESUS' EARTHLY LIFE

To begin with, the title is connected with the earthly life of Jesus Christ. We find that Jesus said that the Son of Man had no place to call home.

Matthew records the following.

> Jesus told him, "Foxes have dens and birds of the sky have nests, but the Son of Man has no place to lay His head" (Matthew 8:20 HCSB).

In this context, there does not seem to be any special meaning to the use of "Son of Man."

2. IT IS USED IN CONTEXTS WHERE JESUS CLAIMS DEITY

Yet we find this designation used in contexts when Jesus' deity is being claimed. For example, we read in Matthew how Jesus used this description of Himself when He claimed the ability to forgive sins.

> But that you may know that the Son of Man has authority on earth to forgive sins—he said to the paralytic— (Mark 2:10 ESV).

Here Jesus claims authority to forgive sins while using the title "Son of Man" when referring to Himself. Forgiveness of sins is something which only God can do. Interestingly, Jesus claimed this authority but used the title "Son of Man" rather than "Son of God."

We also find that Jesus claimed that He, the Son of Man, was "Lord of the Sabbath." Mark records Him saying the following.

> Therefore the Son of man is Lord also of the sabbath (Mark 2:28 KJV).

Again, we find this designation of Himself used in a context of rights and privileges which belong to God alone. Indeed, only God Himself could claim that He is Lord of the Sabbath.

Jesus gave the reason for His coming to earth. In doing so, He again called Himself the "Son of Man." We read in Luke.

And I, the Son of Man, have come to seek and save those like him who are lost (Luke 19:10 NLT).

God the Son, Jesus Christ, came to earth to save the lost. Again we find that Jesus used this title "Son of Man" of Himself— rather than Messiah, or "Son of God."

3. THE TITLE IS CONNECTED WITH JESUS' SUFFERINGS

We also discover that the "Son of Man" is connected with the sufferings that Jesus would experience on behalf of humanity. We read that Jesus used this title when He began to predict what would happen to Him in the future.

Then He began to teach them that the Son of Man must suffer many things, and be rejected by the elders, the chief priests, and the scribes, be killed, and rise after three days (Mark 8:31 HCSB).

Therefore, Jesus used the title "Son of Man" when referring to His suffering on the cross, as well as His resurrection. Again, we do not find the Lord referring to Himself with His other titles, Son of God or Messiah, when predicting these coming events.

4. THIS SPEAKS OF JESUS' EXALTATION AND RULE

The title "Son of Man" also has to do with his exaltation and rule over humanity. Jesus used this title when He spoke of His return to the earth and His rule.

But when the Son of Man comes in his glory, and all the angels with him, then he will sit upon his glorious throne (Matthew 25:31 NLT).

Jesus will rule and reign as the Son of Man. Once again, this is His favorite title.

These are the various ways in which the title "Son of Man" is used by Jesus. What conclusions should we make about them? How should we understand this phrase?

VIEWPOINT 1: SOME BELIEVE IT REFERS TO JESUS' HUMANITY

Some feel the title "Son of Man" refers to the fact that Jesus was perfect humanity. He, as God, came down and lived among us as the perfect human being. By doing this, He fulfilled the Law of Moses and did what no other human being was able to do. By using this title, He is identifying with the people He had come to save.

Therefore, it seems that by using the title "Son of Man" Jesus wanted to convey the truth that He was entirely human. Although He is God Almighty, He became a human being and lived among us for a short period of time. This is the mystery of the incarnation. This is why Jesus preferred the title "Son of Man."

VIEWPOINT 2: OTHERS BELIEVE IT REFERS TO HIS DEITY

There is another point of view which sees the title "Son of Man" as meaning much more than Jesus' humanity.

Indeed, in the Book of Daniel, we read of the prediction that the Son of Man would inherit God's everlasting kingdom. We read the following.

> In my vision at night I looked, and there before me was one like a son of man, coming with the clouds of heaven. He approached the Ancient of Days and was led into his presence. He was given authority, glory and sovereign power; all peoples, nations and men of every language worshiped him. His dominion is an everlasting dominion that will not pass away, and his kingdom is one that will never be destroyed (Daniel 7:13,14 NIV).

In this context, the Son of Man is a divine Person who is in the presence of the Ancient of Days—a designation for God the Father. Obviously this cannot refer to an ordinary human being. Indeed, no human being could be in such a position.

Therefore, Jesus, by the using title, "the Son of Man" was actually claiming deity. This seems to be a better understanding of the term.

Furthermore, it fits with the various contexts in Jesus' public ministry where He used "Son of Man" to claim certain rights which belong to God alone.

JESUS EMPLOYED THE DESIGNATION AT HIS TRIAL

There is something else. When Jesus was on trial for His life, and was asked if He were the Messiah, He referred to this prediction in Daniel.

> Jesus answered him, "Yes, I am. But I can guarantee that from now on you will see the Son of Man in the highest position in heaven. He will be coming on the clouds of heaven" (Matthew 26:64 God's Word).

This statement infuriated the religious rulers. They accused Him of blasphemy for claiming equal authority with God. It was clear to them that Jesus referred to Daniel's prophecy and hence was claiming to have authority to sit on right hand, or the position of authority, with God.

If they understood Jesus was claiming equality with God, then we should understand His claims in the same manner. Consequently, it seems best to view the title "Son of Man" as a reference to Jesus' deity.

SUMMARY TO QUESTION 21
WHY DID JESUS CALL HIMSELF THE SON OF MAN?

The Son of Man is a title that was used exclusively by Jesus Christ. Indeed, His disciples never addressed Him as such. Why did Jesus use this particular title of Himself more than other rightful titles such as the "Son of God" "the Messiah" or the "Son of David?" He certainly was all of these things.

Some believed that Jesus used this particular title to emphasize His humanity. In calling Himself the Son of Man, Christ called attention to the fact that He was a weak, lowly human being. In other words, though He was God Himself, He humbled Himself to become one of us. The title "Son of Man" reflects that humility.

However, this is not the case at all. The title "Son of Man" actually goes back to the Book of Daniel. This Son of Man would inherit the everlasting kingdom of God. Therefore, it is a designation for one who will inherit God's kingdom. In the context of Daniel, it speaks of someone who could freely enter the presence of God the Father. In other words, it speaks of deity.

Indeed, at His trial, Jesus acknowledged that He indeed was the Son of Man—the one who would bring in God's everlasting kingdom. When the religious leaders heard this, they accused Him of blasphemy. Indeed, they accused Him of making Himself equal with God. These leaders, schooled in the Old Testament Scriptures, knew what He was claiming

Consequently, the Son of Man is not merely a title for a human being. Indeed, it is a title which belongs to God Himself.

Did Jesus Ever Sin?

When we talk about the subject of sin we are referring to breaking the law of God. If Jesus had broken the law in any respect, then He would be a sinner. Did Jesus ever sin? Was He ever guilty of breaking God's law? What does the Bible say?

JESUS DID NOT SIN

The Bible answers this question in the clearest of terms. It says that Jesus never once sinned. This is verified by the testimony of the angel Gabriel, the demons, unbelievers, believers, Jesus Himself, and God the Father.

We can make the following observations.

1. THE TESTIMONY OF THE ANGEL GABRIEL AS TO JESUS' SINLESSNESS

To begin with, the angel Gabriel testified to Jesus' sinless nature when he announced the coming birth of the Christ Child to Mary.

> The angel answered her, "The Holy Spirit will come to you, and the power of the Most High will overshadow you. Therefore, the holy child developing inside you will be called the Son of God" (Luke 1:35 God's Word).

This description was never given of any other child that has ever been born. Indeed, this is the only baby which has ever been born who can be rightly be described as "the Holy Child, "the Son of God."

2. THE DEMONS GAVE TESTIMONY OF JESUS' IDENTITY

During His public ministry, we also find that demons, evil angels, testify to the character of Jesus. Indeed, they recognized that He was the Holy One of God. Mark records them saying.

> What do you want with us, Jesus of Nazareth? Have you come to destroy us? I know who you are—the Holy One of God (Mark 1:24 NIV).

They never said this of any human being—no matter how righteous they acted. Jesus alone was the "Holy One" of God.

3. EVEN UNBELIEVERS ACKNOWLEDGED JESUS' IDENTITY

There were a number of unbelievers who gave testimony to Jesus' sinlessness. They include: The Pharisees, the false witnesses at His trial, Pontius Pilate, Pilate's wife, Herod Antipas, the man who died next to Jesus, the centurion who presided over Jesus' death, and Judas Iscariot. The evidence is as follows.

A. THE PHARISEES COULD NOT TRAP HIM IN SIN

The enemies of Jesus, the Pharisees, attempted to trap Him by trying to use something which He said against Him. We read.

> Then the Pharisees went and plotted how to trap Him by what He said (Matthew 22:15 HCSB).

Yet they were unable to catch Him committing any sin.

B. THERE WERE FALSE WITNESSES AT HIS TRIAL

At Jesus' trial, those intimately involved in the proceedings admitted they could find no fault in Him. We read of what they were trying to accomplish in their accusations of Jesus.

> The chief priests and the whole Sanhedrin were looking for false evidence against Jesus so that they could put

him to death. But they did not find any, though many false witnesses came forward. Finally two came forward (Matthew 26:59,60 NIV).

How ironic. Even the false witnesses could not find any sin in Him!

C. PONTIUS PILATE DECLARED JESUS INNOCENT

Pontius Pilate, the Roman governor of Judea, declared the innocence of Jesus after he had examined him.

Pilate went back out and said, "I don't find this man guilty of anything!" (John 18:38 CEV).

Jesus never said or did anything that could be called sinful.

Later, Pilate again told the crowd Jesus was innocent. John records him saying.

Pilate went outside again and said to the people, "I am going to bring him out to you now, but understand clearly that I find him not guilty" (John 19:4 NLT).

The man who sentenced Jesus to death realized that He was not guilty.

D. THE WIFE OF PILATE ADDS HER TESTIMONY

Pilate's wife testified that Jesus was a righteous man. Matthew records what she said to her husband as Jesus was on trial.

While he was sitting on the judgment seat, his wife sent to him, saying, "Have nothing to do with that just Man, for I have suffered many things in a dream because of Him" (Matthew 27:19 NKJV).

Though an unbeliever, she realized Jesus was innocent.

E. HEROD ANTIPAS DID NOT BELIEVE JESUS SHOULD DIE

Herod Antipas, the ruler of Judea, did not think Jesus was worthy of death. Pilate said to the religious rulers.

> And said to them, "You brought me this man as one who was inciting the people to rebellion. I have examined him in your presence and have found no basis for your charges against him. Neither has Herod, for he sent him back to us; as you can see, he has done nothing to deserve death" (Luke 23:14,15 NIV).

Herod, like Pilate, found no wrong in Jesus.

F. THE CRIMINAL NEXT TO JESUS ON THE CROSS SAW HIS INNOCENCE

Jesus died on the cross between two criminals. One of them recognized Jesus' innocence. He said to the other dying criminal.

> We deserve to die for our evil deeds, but this man hasn't done anything wrong (Luke 23:41 NLT).

The criminal could see the difference between Jesus and himself. He recognized his guilt—as well as Jesus' innocence.

G. THE CENTURION WHO WATCHED JESUS DIE REALIZED HE WAS INNOCENT

The centurion who presided over Jesus' crucifixion recognized Jesus as someone special. Luke records his response to Jesus' death.

> When the centurion saw what happened, he began to glorify God, saying, "This man really was righteous!" (Luke 23:47 HCSB).

The centurion must have presided over many crucifixions. He could see that Jesus was different than anyone else whom had ever been put to death.

H. THE BETRAYER JUDAS REALIZED JESUS' INNOCENCE

The betrayer of Jesus Christ, Judas Iscariot, realized that he had betrayed someone who was innocent. Matthew records the following conversation between Judas and the religious rulers.

> "I have sinned," he declared, "for I have betrayed an innocent man." "What do we care?" they retorted. "That's your problem" (Matthew 27:4 NLT).

Even sinful Judas knew Jesus was innocent.

Therefore, we find that unbelievers could not find sin in Jesus.

4. THE TESTIMONY OF BELIEVERS ABOUT JESUS' SINLESSNESS

The Scripture also records the attitude of those who believed in Jesus. They make it clear that He was sinless. The Bible records the following testimonies.

A. JOHN THE BAPTIST

John the Baptist, the forerunner of the Messiah, testified to the fact that Jesus was without sin. We read of this in Matthew's gospel as he records the baptism of Jesus.

> Then Jesus went from Galilee to the Jordan River to be baptized by John. But John didn't want to baptize him. "I am the one who needs to be baptized by you," he said, "so why are you coming to me?" But Jesus said, "It must be done, because we must do everything that is right" So then John baptized him. After his baptism, as Jesus came up out of the water, the heavens were opened and he saw the Spirit of God descending like a dove and settling on him (Matthew 3:13-16 NLT).

John realized that it was not necessary to baptize Jesus in water. The reason—Jesus, the Messiah, was without sin.

B. PETER

In his first letter to the believers, Simon Peter testified that Jesus Christ never committed any type of sin. He wrote.

He never sinned, and he never deceived anyone (1 Peter 2:22 NLT).

Peter spent three years constantly watching Jesus. In all of that time, though he saw Him in every conceivable circumstance, Peter never saw Jesus sin.

C. JOHN

The Apostle John, another one of Jesus' disciples, testified that Jesus was without sin. He wrote the following.

But you know that he appeared so that he might take away our sins. And in him is no sin (1 John 3:5 NIV).

John, like Peter, knew Jesus intimately for the three years of His public ministry. While he saw him day and night, He too testified Jesus was without sin.

D. PAUL

The Apostle Paul reported that Jesus was sinless. When he wrote his second letter to the Corinthians, he put it this way.

For God made Christ, who never sinned, to be the offering for our sin, so that we could be made right with God through Christ (2 Corinthians 5:21 NLT).

Paul made it clear that Jesus was without sin.

E. THE TESTIMONY OF THE EARLY CHURCH

When the early church gathered to pray, they recognized the holiness of the Lord Jesus. We read what they said in the Book of Acts.

Here in Jerusalem, Herod and Pontius Pilate got together with the Gentiles and the people of Israel. Then they turned against your holy Servant Jesus, your chosen Messiah. . . Show your mighty power, as we heal people and work miracles and wonders in the name of your holy Servant Jesus (Acts 4:27,30 CEV).

The church testified to the sinlessness of Jesus. Many of these people had observed Him during His earthly ministry. They, like Jesus' inner circle of disciples, had never seen Him sin.

F. THE WRITER TO THE HEBREWS

The writer to the Hebrews testified that while Jesus Christ was indeed tempted, He did not give in to sin. We read.

For we do not have a High Priest who cannot sympathize with our weaknesses, but was in all points tempted as we are, yet without sin (Hebrews 4:15 NKJV).

To be the heavenly High Priest for believers, Jesus had to be sinless.

JESUS' DISCIPLES WERE CONSTANTLY WITH HIM

Again, we want to emphasize that the testimony of Jesus' disciples is especially significant. Indeed, it was given by some of the very same people who were constantly with Jesus. They saw Him when He was tired, they saw Him when He was hungry, they saw Him when the multitudes pressed around Him.

Yet they testified that in all this they never once had seen Him sin. Their testimony, that He was without sin, carries considerable weight because they honestly reported their own faults and shortcomings.

5. JESUS' OWN TESTIMONY ABOUT HIS SINLESSNESS

As we examine the account of the life of Jesus Christ, as recorded in the New Testament, we observe that He believed Himself to be without sin. When He came to be baptized by John the Baptist, Jesus was momentarily stopped because John realized it was unnecessary. Matthew records what happened as follows.

> Then Jesus appeared. He came from Galilee to the Jordan River to be baptized by John. But John tried to stop him and said, "I need to be baptized by you. Why are you coming to me" (Matthew 3:14 God's Word).

John's baptism was for the confession of sin—but he realized that this One had no sin. However, Jesus insisted upon being baptized. We read.

> But Jesus said, "It must be done, because we must do everything that is right." So then John baptized him (Matthew 3:15 NLT).

Jesus submitted to the baptism but did not confess sin—for He had no sin.

A. JESUS DID NOT GIVE IN TO TEMPTATION

Immediately after His baptism, Satan tempted Christ. Yet, Jesus refused to give in to the temptation. He told the devil.

> Jesus said to him, "Away with you, Satan! for it is written, 'Worship the Lord your God, and serve only him'" (Matthew 4:10 NRSV).

In the great spiritual battle with the devil, Jesus did not yield to sin.

We also discover the following things about Jesus' testimony to His lack of sin.

B. HE CHALLENGED PEOPLE TO FIND SIN IN HIM

Throughout His ministry Jesus challenged those with Him to find sin in His life. He made the following public challenge.

Which of you can truthfully accuse me of sin? And since I am telling you the truth, why don't you believe me? (John 8:46 NLT).

The response from those surrounding Him was silence. They had never seen Him sin—for He had not sinned. Jesus claimed absolute sinlessness. Indeed, He was never conscious of any personal sin.

C. JESUS OFFERED NO SACRIFICE FOR SIN

Although Jesus Christ perfectly kept the Mosaic Law, we never find Him offering a sacrifice for sin. He daily taught in the temple yet never offered a sacrifice while He was there. The writer to the Hebrews describes His holy character in this manner.

> We need a chief priest who is holy, innocent, pure, set apart from sinners, and who has the highest position in heaven. We need a priest who doesn't have to bring daily sacrifices as those chief priests did. First they brought sacrifices for their own sins, and then they brought sacrifices for the sins of the people. Jesus brought the sacrifice for the sins of the people once and for all when he sacrificed himself (Hebrews 7:26,27 God's Word).

Jesus brought no sacrifice for sin, Instead He sacrificed Himself. This is another indication that He had no sin.

D. JESUS DID NOT NEED THE NEW BIRTH

Jesus told the religious leader Nicodemus that everyone needed to be "born again" or "born from above." We read in John.

> Jesus replied, "I assure you: Unless someone is born again, he cannot see the kingdom of God" (John 3:3 HCSB).

However, Jesus never indicated that He needed the new birth. This was something which everyone else had to have.

E. JESUS PRAYED ON BEHALF OF OTHERS FOR THEIR FORGIVENESS

Jesus prayed for the forgiveness of others. The Lord predicted that Simon Peter would deny knowing Him on that very night Peter. Yet Jesus also said that He would pray for him. We read.

> Then the Lord said, "Simon, Simon, listen! Satan has demanded to have you apostles for himself. He wants to separate you from me as a farmer separates wheat from husks. But I have prayed for you, Simon, that your faith will not fail. So when you recover, strengthen the other disciples" (Luke 22:31,32 God's Word).

Therefore, Jesus would pray for the failure of Peter. While we find Jesus praying for others, we never find Him asking others to pray for Him for any sin, or lack of faith.

F. JESUS OFFERED NO PRAYER FOR FORGIVENESS

In addition, we never find Jesus praying for forgiveness for Himself. Although a number of His prayers are recorded, we never find Him even hinting that He had committed sin.

At the end of His life, while proceeding to the Garden of Gethsemane to be betrayed by Judas Iscariot, Jesus prayed to His Heavenly Father and said the following.

> I have glorified You on the earth by completing the work You gave Me to do (John 17:4 HCSB).

Knowing of His impending death, His prayer was not one of confession, but rather one of victory. Jesus had finished the mission given to Him by God the Father, and He had finished it without committing a sin.

On the cross, the Lord Jesus asked His Father to forgive those who crucified Him. Luke records Him saying.

Jesus said, "Father, forgive them, for they do not know what they are doing." And they divided up his clothes by casting lots (Luke 23:34 NIV).

However, He never asked forgiveness for Himself.

G. JESUS SAID GOD WAS HIS FATHER, NOT HIS SAVIOR

We find that Jesus called God His Father, but He never referred to Him as His Savior. Why? It is because Jesus needed no Savior.

Indeed, He claimed to do only those things that pleased the Father. John records Him saying.

> And the one who sent me is with me—he has not deserted me. For I always do those things that are pleasing to him (John 8:29 NLT).

Note that Jesus said that He "always" did the things which pleased the Father.

Our Lord also claimed that He kept His Father's commandments. We also read about this in the Gospel of John. He said.

> If you obey my commandments, you will live in my love. I have obeyed my Father's commandments, and in that way I live in his love (John 15:10 God's Word).

Clearly, Jesus believed that He was without sin.

6. THE TESTIMONY OF GOD THE FATHER CONCERNING JESUS' SINLESSNESS

By far, the most significant testimony that Jesus was sinless came from God the Father. We find that He testified to the sinlessness of Christ on a number of occasions.

A. THE FATHER VERBALLY ACKNOWLEDGED THE SON

At Jesus' baptism, the Father verbally testified to the character of the Son. Indeed, He voiced His pleasure of the Son.

> And the Holy Spirit descended on Him in a physical appearance like a dove. And a voice came from heaven: You are My beloved Son. I take delight in You! (Luke 3:22 HCSB).

The Father was well-pleased with the Son.

Later in His ministry, at the Transfiguration, the Father again voiced audibly that the Son had pleased Him.

> While he was still speaking, a bright cloud enveloped them, and a voice from the cloud said, "This is my Son, whom I love; with him I am well pleased. Listen to him!" (Matthew 17:5 NIV).

In front of some of Jesus' disciples, the Father again expressed His pleasure with Jesus.

On another occasion, before the multitude, the Father testified to the ministry of the Son before the crowd. Jesus prayed to the Father.

> "Father, glorify Your name." Then a voice came from heaven, saying, "I have both glorified it and will glorify it again" (John 12:28 NKJV).

Again, we have an audible testimony by God the Father to God the Son.

B. THE FATHER ACCEPTED JESUS' SACRIFICE

The final act that demonstrated the testimony of God the Father to the sinlessness of Jesus, God the Son, was the acceptance of His sacrifice on the cross. The fact that He received Jesus into heaven showed that His mission was accomplished as the perfect, sinless sacrifice. Jesus' last words were recorded by Luke.

And Jesus called out with a loud voice, "Father, into Your hands I entrust My spirit." Saying this, He breathed His last (Luke 23:46 HCSB).

If Jesus had sinned in any manner, then He would not have been able to appear in the presence of His Father. The Father's unqualified acceptance of Jesus Christ was the final testimony to His sinlessness.

7. THE TESTIMONY OF THE LAW (HE WAS THE PERFECT SACRIFICE)

There is something else which we must appreciate. The Old Testament sacrifices gave a foreshadowing of Christ's sacrifice on Calvary's cross. The Scripture was very specific about the requirements for the sacrifice.

A. THE ANIMAL SACRIFICES HAD TO BE WITHOUT BLEMISH

The animal that was to be offered was to be without any blemish to be accepted. This is made clear in the Book of Leviticus. It says.

When anyone brings from the herd or flock a fellowship offering to the LORD to fulfill a special vow or as a freewill offering, it must be without defect or blemish to be acceptable (Leviticus 22:21 NIV).

A blemished animal was not acceptable.

Moses also wrote elsewhere about the requirements for sacrifice. He again made it plain that the sacrifice had to be without defect. We read.

This is a requirement of the law that the LORD has commanded: Tell the Israelites to bring you a red heifer without defect or blemish and that has never been under a yoke (Numbers 19:2 NIV).

No defect, no blemish. Only animals which were unblemished could be sacrificed.

We also read in the Book of Numbers about the necessity of the animals not having any physical defect. The Bible explains it in this manner.

> Say to them: When you present your daily whole burnt offerings to the LORD, you must offer two one-year-old male lambs with no physical defects. . . On the Sabbath day, sacrifice two one-year-old male lambs with no physical defects. They must be accompanied by a grain offering of three quarts of choice flour mixed with olive oil, and a drink offering. This is the whole burnt offering to be presented each Sabbath day, in addition to the regular daily burnt offering and its accompanying drink offering. . . On the first day of each month, present an extra burnt offering to the LORD of two young bulls, one ram, and seven one-year-old male lambs, all with no physical defects" (Numbers 28:3,9,11 NLT).

Again we have the emphasis that the sacrifices had to be without any defect, or blemish. They had to be as perfect as they possibly could be. This is what the Lord demanded.

B. JESUS WAS WITHOUT BLEMISH

The New Testament reported that Jesus Himself was without blemish. The writer to the Hebrews made this comparison of Jesus with the Old Testament requirements for sacrifice. He explained it in the following manner.

> The blood of goats and bulls and the ashes of a heifer sprinkled on those who are ceremonially unclean sanctify them so that they are outwardly clean. How much more, then, will the blood of Christ, who through the eternal Spirit offered himself unblemished to God, cleanse our consciences from acts that lead to death, so that we may serve the living God! (Hebrews 9:13,14 NIV).

Jesus was perfect in every way. He was the unblemished sacrifice which was offered up to God the Father.

Simon Peter, in his first letter to the believers, emphasized that Jesus Christ was a lamb without blemish or defect. He put it this way to his readers.

> Realize that you weren't set free from the worthless life handed down to you from your ancestors by a payment of silver or gold which can be destroyed. Rather, the payment that freed you was the precious blood of Christ, the lamb with no defects or imperfections (1 Peter 1:18,19 God's Word).

Therefore, to be the perfect sacrifice for the sins of the human race, Jesus had to be without sin. There could be no blemish of any kind on His character.

Consequently, from every source, friendly and unfriendly, the testimony is unanimous—Jesus Christ never sinned. Therefore, we conclude that Jesus indeed lived a sinless life while here upon the earth.

SUMMARY TO QUESTION 22
DID JESUS EVER SIN?

There is the issue as to whether or not Jesus Christ ever committed a sin while He was here upon the earth. Scripture is clear that He did not. The evidence is as follows.

First, before Jesus was born, the angel Gabriel, in announcing Jesus' conception, made it clear that He would be the, "Holy One of God."

We have another testimony to Jesus' sinlessness, from the demons. When confronted by Jesus, they confessed to Him that He was without sin.

There is another witness—Jesus' own enemies testified to the fact that He was without sin. During His public ministry, we find that several unbelievers admitted that Jesus was sinless.

To begin with, the religious leaders, the Pharisees, attempted to trap Jesus in His words. But they could not find anything sinful in what He said.

The false witnesses at Jesus' trial could not find anything with which to accuse Him. Pontius Pilate said that he could find no fault in Jesus. The wife of Pilate also warned her husband not to harm this righteous man. The king, Herod Antipas, also acknowledged Jesus' sinlessness. One of the two criminals which was crucified next to Jesus recognized His sinlessness. We also find that the centurion presiding over Jesus' crucifixion doing the same thing. He knew they were crucifying a righteous man.

Finally, the traitor Judas Iscariot recognized that he had betrayed an innocent man. Therefore, the enemies of Jesus give testimony to His sinlessness.

We also find that the friends of Jesus testifying to His sinlessness. John the Baptist, the forerunner of Jesus, did not want to baptize Him because he knew the Lord was without sin.

In addition, the disciples of Jesus, those who spent three years in constant ministry with Him, testified that they had never seen Him sin.

This, of course, is extremely significant for they were with Him day and night in all sorts of circumstances. If He had any sin, He would not have been able to hide it from them.

In addition, there is the testimony of the Apostle Paul. He made it clear that Jesus committed no sin whatsoever.

There is also the witness of Jesus Himself to His own sinlessness. From the beginning of His life, until the very end, He made it plain that He was without sin. Since Jesus never lied about anything, we can be confident that He was telling the truth about His own sinless nature.

The most significant testimony we have is that of God the Father. Two things stand out.

First, God the Father verbally acknowledged Jesus' sinlessness at His baptism, as well as at His transfiguration.

Furthermore, the fact that He accepted Jesus' sacrifice on the cross shows that Jesus was indeed the sinless Savior.

This is consistent with what the Old Testament taught about the need for an unblemished sacrifice to be offered. Jesus was that unblemished, sinless sacrifices.

In sum, from all sources we find that Jesus was without sin.

Could Jesus Have Sinned?
(The Peccability Of Christ)

There is an age-old question that has been discussed among believers and unbelievers alike with respect to the sinfulness of Jesus. Was He able to sin? Could He do something wrong— or was this something impossible for Him to do? What does the Bible say?

The view that Christ could have sinned is called, "peccability" (from the Latin term meaning "sin"). This position states that Christ's human nature was susceptible to sin. There are three ways in which this view is expressed. They are as follows.

VIEW 1: CHRIST HAD A SINFUL NATURE AND DID SIN

Liberal Christians, as well as unbelievers, believe that Jesus Christ possessed a nature that could sin and did sin. They do not seem Him as different from any other human being in that respect.

RESPONSE

The Scripture is very clear that Jesus did not sin. If a person takes the New Testament seriously, they cannot hold the position of Christ's sinfulness. Consequently, for Bible-believers, this is not an option.

VIEW 2: CHRIST HAD A SINFUL NATURE BUT DID NOT SIN

There are those who held that God the Son, Jesus Christ, had a sinful nature when He was here upon the earth but He overcame it by the power of the Holy Spirit. This false doctrine is based on a misunderstanding of Romans 8:3, which reads as follows.

> For what the law could not do, in that it was weak through the flesh, God sending his own Son in the likeness of sinful flesh, and for sin, condemned sin in the flesh (Romans 8:3 KJV).

The idea that Christ came in the "likeness of sinful humanity" caused some to believe that He Himself had a sin nature. The Bible does not teach this.

Furthermore, this has a mistaken idea of human nature. Human nature does not have to be sinful. When God created Adam and Eve, He created them with a human nature that was sinless. Likewise, Jesus' human nature was without sin. In fact, Jesus was called the last Adam.

> The Scriptures tell us, "The first man, Adam, became a living person." But the last Adam—that is, Christ—is a life-giving Spirit (1 Corinthians 15:45 NLT).

He was the last human to have a sinless nature.

VIEW 3: HE DID NOT HAVE A SINFUL NATURE, COULD HAVE SINNED, BUT DID NOT

It is also widely believed that Jesus Christ could have sinned, but did not. Though He was fully God, the fact that He was also human meant that He potentially could have sinned. Since the Bible says that Christ was tempted, it proves that He could have sinned. Jesus Christ, as this theory goes, could not have been a sympathetic High Priest to us when we are tempted unless He himself could have sinned.

This sums up the three main theories with respect to the idea that Jesus Christ could have sinned.

SUMMARY TO QUESTION 23
COULD JESUS HAVE SINNED? (THE PECCABILITY OF CHRIST)

The idea of Christ's peccability means that He was able to sin when He was here upon the earth. Basically, three different views are expressed from this position.

One theory holds that Christ could have sinned and did sin. This, however, has no basis whatsoever in the New Testament. Those who hold this perspective do not take the Bible seriously in what it has to say about Jesus. Thus, Bible-believers reject this idea.

Another theory is that Jesus Christ had a sinful nature but overcame it by the power of the Holy Spirit. It is assumed in this argument that to be a human being, then one must have a sinful nature.

But this is not the case at all. Indeed, having a human nature does not mean that Christ had a sinful nature. In fact, Adam and Eve had human natures when they were created, but each of them was without sin until the time they decided to rebel against God.

The main theory of Christ's peccability is that He was fully human without a sinful nature— yet it was possible for Him to sin. Although it is admitted that He did not sin, it is claimed that the possibility was still there. There are many Bible-believers who hold to this theory.

This is a brief summation of the three main views held by those who believe that Jesus could have sinned.

Was It Impossible For Jesus To Sin? (Impeccability)

While all Bible-believing Christians agree that Jesus did not sin, there is the view that He was incapable of sinning while here upon the earth. This is known, as His "impeccability." The word comes from the Latin. It means, "no sin."

THE CASE FOR IMPECCABILITY

Those who argue that Jesus Christ could not have sinned do so for the following reasons.

1. THE DUAL NATURE OF JESUS – GOD CANNOT BE TEMPTED TO SIN

While God the Son, Jesus Christ, had a human nature, He also had a divine nature. Since He was the eternal God who became a human being, it was impossible for the divine nature to sin.

In addition, the human nature could not act apart from the divine nature. Therefore, He could not sin. James wrote the following words.

> Don't blame God when you are tempted! God cannot be tempted by evil, and he doesn't use evil to tempt others. We are tempted by our own desires that drag us off and trap us. Our desires make us sin, and when sin is finished with us, it leaves us dead (James 1:13-15 CEV).

Since God cannot be tempted to sin, Jesus could not sin. Therefore, the issue as to whether Christ could or could not sin is solved by this fact.

2. CHRIST HAS AN UNCHANGING NATURE

There is more. The Bible says that Jesus Christ is unchangeable, He always remains the same. The writer to the Hebrews said.

> Jesus Christ the same yesterday, and today, and forever (Hebrews 13:8 KJV).

Since Jesus Christ is God, and God cannot sin in any way, then Jesus could not have sinned in any way. The nature of God does not change. If Jesus could have sinned while on the earth, then it would be possible for Him to sin in heaven. This is a second reason as to why Christ could not have committed sin.

3. CHRIST IS ALL-POWERFUL (OMNIPOTENT)

One of the attributes of God is that He is all-powerful, or omnipotent. Jesus did not give up this attribute when He became human. Indeed, Jesus Himself said that He had been given "all authority." We read.

> Jesus came to them and said: I have been given all authority in heaven and on earth! (Matthew 28:18 CEV).

Because God is all-powerful, He has no weaknesses whatsoever. This would include a weakness to sin.

4. JESUS IS ALL-KNOWING

In addition, Scripture says that Jesus Christ is all-knowing. John wrote.

> Then Jesus, knowing all that would happen to him, came forward and said to them, "Whom do you seek" (John 18:4 ESV).

The disciples also recognized that Jesus was aware of everything.

Now we know that you know all things and do not need anyone to question you; this is why we believe that you came from God (John 16:30 ESV).

Since Jesus is all-knowing, He could not have been deceived into committing a sin. This includes hypothetical situations—for Jesus knew all things that have happened and could possibly happen.

For example, He knew what would have happened to certain cities in the past, such as Tyre and Sidon—had they repented.

> Woe to you, Chorazin! Woe to you, Bethsaida! For if the miracles that were done in you had been done in Tyre and Sidon, they would have repented in sackcloth and ashes long ago! (Matthew 11:21 HCSB).

The New Living Translation puts it this way.

> What horrors await you, Korazin and Bethsaida! For if the miracles I did in you had been done in wicked Tyre and Sidon, their people would have sat in deep repentance long ago, clothed in sackcloth and throwing ashes on their heads to show their remorse (Matthew 11:21 NLT).

Jesus knew what would have happened to the ancient cities of Tyre and Sidon had they repented of their sin. Though these cities did not repent, Jesus stated what would have occurred had they done so. This shows that He knew "all things."

5. THE NATURE OF THE TEMPTATIONS

Another point concerns the nature of the temptations of Christ Jesus. The nature of Christ's temptation came from without—not from within. For sin to occur there must be an inward response to the outward temptation. Since Jesus did not possess a sin nature, there was no possibility of Him to respond to the temptation.

THE UNIQUENESS OF HIS TEMPTATIONS MUST BE CONSIDERED

The uniqueness of Jesus' temptation must also be kept in mind. We find that there were only three individuals in Scripture who experienced unique temptations—Adam, Eve, and Jesus.

Adam and Eve, unfortunately, gave in to the temptation and brought sin into the world. Jesus, on the other hand, resisted the temptation. They are the only three people who came into this world without a sin nature.

A. THESE TESTS WERE UNIQUE TO JESUS

Yet Jesus was unique from Adam and Eve. He was no ordinary man. No ordinary human being would ever be tempted in the ways which Jesus Christ, God the Son, was tempted. Indeed, none of us could ever be tempted to turn stones into bread, or prove that we are the Messiah by jumping from a high place. Neither would any human being be offered all the kingdoms of the world if they simply bowed down to Satan. These particular tests were designed for Jesus only. In other words, they were uniquely given to Him.

THEY COVERED ALL AREAS THAT ARE COMMON TO ALL HUMANS

Although the specific tests in which Jesus was subjected were unique to Him, they do represent temptations that are common to humankind. The Apostle John said that sin could be placed in the following categories

> The lust of the flesh, the lust of the eyes, and the pride in one's lifestyle—is not from the Father, but is from the world (1 John 2:16 HCSB).

The temptations that Jesus experienced fall into these categories. He was tempted or tested in each of these areas—yet He did not sin.

IN WHAT SENSE WAS JESUS TESTED IN ALL THINGS?

The writer to the Hebrews emphasizes that Jesus was tested in all things. He wrote.

> For we do not have a high priest who is unable to sympathize with our weaknesses, but we have one who has been tempted in every way, just as we are—yet was without sin (Hebrews 4:15 NIV).

This means that Jesus experienced tests that are representative of every category of tests that human's experience. It does not mean that He experienced each individual temptation which we will be tempted with. He did not.

Consequently, the temptations of Jesus were real and met a real purpose. Yet in all of this, there was no possibility that He could sin—according to this perspective.

WHY THEN THE TEMPTATIONS?

Finally, there is the purpose of the temptations of Jesus Christ. The reason He was tempted was not to see whether or not He could sin. Indeed, the purpose was to show that He could *not* sin. It was to demonstrate that He could not succumb in any way to the temptations that were put in His path. The outcome was never in doubt.

SUMMARY TO QUESTION 24
WAS IT IMPOSSIBLE FOR JESUS TO SIN? (IMPECCABILITY)

While there are those people who argue that God the Son, Jesus Christ, could have sinned while He was in a human body here upon the earth, there are those which believe that Jesus could not have sinned. This is known as the "impeccability of Christ." Those who hold this position put forth a number of reasons as to why they believe this.

One reason is based upon His nature as Almighty God. Jesus, as God, could not have sinned. Since He was fully God, as well as fully human while He was here on the earth, this makes the idea of sin something which was impossible. God cannot sin! This fact ends the discussion for many people.

We are also told that Jesus Christ had an unchanging nature. This is another reason to believe that He could not sin. Indeed, His divine nature is impossible to change in any way.

Some argue the fact that Christ was both all-powerful and all-knowing precludes Him from being able to sin. Since He always knew what was going to occur, He could make certain that He avoided any missteps.

There are those who argue that the nature of the temptations is another reason for the impossibility of Jesus to sin. His temptations did not come from within but rather from outside. Since He was perfect, it was not possible for Him to respond to the temptation.

It must also be appreciated that the temptations were unique to Him—only Jesus could be tempted with certain things. Indeed, none of us will be tempted in exactly the same way as Jesus.

It is also suggested that His temptations were representative of the various things that all humans face. While there is not necessarily a one- to-one correspondence with each testing or temptation which we experience, His temptations or "testings" are of the same nature as what we experience.

Finally, those who hold this position must answer the big question, "Why then the temptations? Why tempt someone who, by definition, could not fail?"

The answer lies in the purpose of these testings. It was not to discover whether or not that He would not fail, but rather to show us that He could not fail. It was to make it clear to all who trust Him that we have a Savior who cannot fail. What He sets out to do, He will do.

This is a brief summation of some of the chief arguments for the impeccability of Jesus Christ.

QUESTION 25

What Are The Usual Objections Brought Up Against The Idea That Jesus Could Not Have Sinned? (His Impeccability)

There continues to be discussions among Bible-believers as to whether or not Jesus Christ had the ability to sin while He was here upon the earth. Many people believe that He could not have sinned. This is known as the "impeccability of Christ."

Of course, if Jesus could not have sinned, then one may ask the question if the temptations that He experienced were genuine. Why test someone who could not fail? What would be the point of it all?

THE COMMON OBJECTIONS AGAINST JESUS' IMPECCABILITY

This leads us to the common objections which are brought up against the idea of whether or not Jesus Christ could sin. The main ones can be simply stated as follows.

1. JESUS MUST NOT HAVE HAD THE POWER OF CHOICE IF HE COULD NOT HAVE SINNED

If it was not possible for God the Son, Jesus Christ, to sin, then it is claimed that He must not have had the power of choice. If He did not have the power of choice, then He was not a real or genuine human being. To be human, one must be able to make legitimate choices. Indeed, we have to make choices between good and bad, right and wrong. Since Jesus was completely human, then this means that theoretically He could have chosen to sin. While Bible-believers admit that He did not sin, this does not mean that He could not have sinned.

2. THE TEMPTATION WAS A FARCE IF HE COULD NOT FAIL

Another common objection concerns the purpose of the temptations which Jesus Christ experienced. If God the Son could not sin while He was here upon the earth, then why was He tempted at all? Wouldn't the temptation be a farce? In what sense can a being be tempted who was not capable of sinning? The whole exercise would be pointless. Some go as far to say that it would be deceptive. Since the Lord does not deceive us, we should assume that the temptations were legitimate.

3. HE CANNOT IDENTITY WITH HUMANITY IF HE COULD NOT SIN

If Jesus Christ could not possibly sin, then how could He identify with humanity? How could He sympathize with our temptations? Seemingly, He could not. Yet we are told that He can indeed identify with us. The writer to the Hebrews emphasized this when he wrote the following.

> For we do not have a high priest who is unable to sympathize
> with our weaknesses, but One who has been tested in every
> way as we are, yet without sin (Hebrews 4:15 HCSB).

The fact that He can sympathize with our weaknesses indicates that His temptations were genuine. While He did not sin, He certainly could have sinned.

This sums up the usual objections to the position that Christ could not sin. While they convince many people, others are unconvinced.

SUMMARY TO QUESTION 25
WHAT ARE THE USUAL OBJECTIONS BROUGHT UP AGAINST THE IDEA THAT JESUS COULD NOT HAVE SINNED? (HIS IMPECCABILITY)

There are many people who hold to the doctrine of the impeccability of Jesus Christ. The idea is that Christ was not able to sin while He was here upon the earth. While His temptations were genuine, there was no possible way in which He could have failed.

As can be imagined, not everyone agrees with this position. One argument concerns Jesus' humanity. If He was genuinely human, then He needed to have the ability to make genuine choices. This means the choice to sin. Though He did not sin, it is argued that He could have chosen to sin.

There is also the question as to the purpose of the temptations Jesus received. It is argued that unless there was some possibility of Jesus choosing to sin, the temptations were not truly genuine. Indeed, why tempt someone with something which they were not able to do? Logically, it follows that He must have at least had the possibility of sinning.

The key verse which is usually brought up is Hebrews 4:15. This verse says that Jesus was tempted or tested in all ways such as we are—yet He did not sin. To many, this indicates that He could have sinned.

These are the usual arguments which are brought up against the idea of Christ's inability to sin—His impeccability.

What Common Ground Do Believers Have With Respect To Christ's Ability To Sin?

Whether or not Jesus Christ was able to commit sin has been an issue which has caused debate among Bible-believers. However, there is some common ground on which believers can agree with respect to the question of Jesus ability or non-ability to sin. They are as follows.

1. THE BIBLE IS SILENT ON THE MATTER OF JESUS' ABILITY TO SIN

The issue of Christ's ability or inability to sin is not something about which the Bible directly comments. It is silent on the matter. Therefore, any solution to the question of what He could, or could not, do has to be decided upon the totality of the biblical teaching upon the subject. In other words, we have to depend upon inferences rather than direct statements from Scripture.

2. JESUS CHRIST DID NOT SIN

Whether or not Jesus could have sinned, the Scriptures make it clear that He did not. All Bible-believing Christians agree on this fact. There is no question that Jesus went through His entire life without breaking God's law in any form. On this point, there is no doubt.

3. JESUS CHRIST HAD TWO NATURES

The Bible also says that Jesus Christ possessed a perfect human nature as well as a divine nature. He was a real human being and was fully divine. This is one of the basic truths of the New Testament to which all believers agree.

4. HIS TEMPTATIONS WERE GENUINE

We can also conclude that the forty-day temptation that Jesus experienced was genuine. Scripture makes it clear that He was fully tested by the devil during that difficult period. Again, the Bible states this in such a way that it is beyond all doubt. Indeed, the Bible emphasizes that the Lord "suffered" while being tempted.

5. HE IS ABLE TO SYMPATHIZE WITH BELIEVERS

Because the temptations were genuine, Jesus is able to sympathize with believers through their temptations. Scripture says that Jesus can personally understand our sufferings and limitations because He went through it Himself.

These are some of things which Bible-believers can agree upon with respect to the various temptations that Jesus received by the devil during his forty days in the wilderness.

SUMMARY TO QUESTION 26
WHAT COMMON GROUND DO BELIEVERS HAVE WITH RESPECT TO CHRIST'S ABILITY TO SIN?

Bible-believers do not agree as to whether or not God the Son, Jesus Christ, could have sinned while He was here upon the earth. Indeed, there are good people on both sides of this issue.

While there is disagreement on this issue, there are a number of things that all believers can agree upon with respect to the temptations of Jesus which He received during His earthly life.

First, the Bible is silent on the matter on His ability to sin. The Scripture does not specifically tell us, one way or the other, as to what He could, or could, not do. Any conclusion which we may reach will be from the overall teaching of Scripture. In other words, it is by inference—not by direct teaching.

Second, whether or not He could have sinned, the evidence is plain that Jesus Christ did not sin. This is something which everyone agrees upon. Nobody could truthfully accuse Him of sin.

Third, Jesus Christ had two natures, one human and one divine. He was fully human and fully divine at the same time. He was the God-man. All Bible-believers are in agreement about this crucial doctrine.

Fourth, the temptations that He experienced were genuine. He truly experienced hunger, thirst, as well as the offer of Satan to bypass the cross. These testings were real!

Finally, He is able to sympathize with believers because of His experience of being tempted. While His individual temptations may not directly correspond with each and everything which we experience, the totality of His being was subjected to similar testings as we experience. This allows Him to identify with us.

While we may not come to complete agreement among ourselves as to whether or not Jesus could have sinned, these five points are something which all Bible-believers can accept.

QUESTION 27

What Was The Purpose
Of Jesus' Temptation?

Three out of the four gospels record the temptation of God the Son, Jesus Christ. In fact, we are told that the Holy Spirit expressly led Jesus into the wilderness for the specific reason to be tempted.

> Then Jesus was led by the Spirit into the wilderness to be tempted by the devil (Matthew 4:1 NET).

The fact of His temptation, or testing, is clear. What is not so obvious is why He was tested. For what purpose or purposes was He tempted?

In answering this question, we can come up with at least five reasons as to why God the Son, Jesus Christ, was tempted by the devil.

1. IT DEMONSTRATED HIS GENUINE HUMANITY

To begin with, the temptations which Jesus received gave indisputable proof of His true humanity. The Bible says.

> For because he himself has suffered when tempted, he is able to help those who are being tempted (Hebrews 2:18 ESV).

The fact that He could be tested showed that Jesus was genuinely human. Only human beings can be tempted or tested. God cannot be. While Jesus was fully God He was also completely human. His temptations testify to this fact.

In addition, we are told that He also suffered when He was tempted. This further indicates not only that He was truly human, but also that the temptations He suffered were real.

2. IT IS AN EXAMPLE TO US

The temptations which He received are part of His example to us as believers in Him. Indeed, we are told to walk as He walked. John wrote.

> Whoever says he abides in him ought to walk in the same way in which he walked (1 John 2:6 ESV).

We are to respond to temptations in the same manner as Jesus. We are to resist them by putting our trust in the God the Father through the power of the Holy Spirit.

3. IT FORMED PART OF HIS PERSONAL DISCIPLESHIP

The temptations of Jesus also formed part of His own personal discipline. In some sense, Jesus learned obedience through the temptation. We read in Hebrews.

> While Jesus was here on earth, he offered prayers and pleadings, with a loud cry and tears, to the one who could deliver him out of death. And God heard his prayers because of his reverence for God. So even though Jesus was God's Son, he learned obedience from the things he suffered. In this way, God qualified him as a perfect High Priest, and he became the source of eternal salvation for all those who obey him (Hebrews 5:7-9 NLT).

Jesus learned obedience in the sense that He personally underwent the limitations of being human. He experienced what it means to be limited, to be tested, as well as to suffer.

4. HE CAN SYMPATHIZE WITH US

The temptations of Jesus helped Him sympathize with the trials and tribulations we experience. The Book of Hebrews again says.

This High Priest of ours understands our weaknesses, for he faced all of the same temptations we do, yet he did not sin (Hebrews 4:15 NLT).

Jesus experienced the same types of temptations that all human beings undergo. Therefore, He can sympathize with humanity.

5. IT IS PART OF THE GREAT CONFLICT

Finally, the temptations of Jesus formed part of the great conflict in which the "seed of woman," God the Son, was to "bruise the head of the serpent"—namely, the devil.

In this first great struggle of this conflict, Jesus was completely victorious. Yet it did not end there. Indeed, this conflict with the devil would take place during His entire public ministry. However, the Bible testifies that He remained victorious in each and every battle which He had with the devil. In other words, Jesus never sinned in any manner.

This sums up some of the reasons as to why Jesus was led to be tempted by the devil.

SUMMARY TO QUESTION 27
WHAT WAS THE PURPOSE FOR JESUS' TEMPTATION?

Three out of the four gospels say that Jesus Christ was led of the Spirit to be tempted by the devil. These various temptations had a purpose. We can make the following observations.

First, these temptations demonstrated His true humanity. Indeed, only human beings can be tempted. The fact that Jesus would submit to temptations, or testings, shows that He was an actual human being. In fact, we are specifically told that He suffered during these temptations.

Jesus also underwent the temptations so as to be an example to us. We are to respond to temptations in the same manner in which He did. As Jesus trusted God the Father through the power of the Holy Spirit to resist the temptations, we should do the same thing when we are tempted. The same Holy Spirit which indwelt Jesus indwells those who believe in Him. Our responsibility is to submit to His control.

In addition, the temptations Jesus experienced were part of His own personal discipleship. He had to take part in the things in which we humans suffer, so as to be the One who would die as our substitute. In other words, He had to experience the things we experience as humans.

The temptations also helped Him to sympathize with us when we are tempted. He has endured the same limitations and sufferings we endure. He can identify with us in our struggles.

Finally, the temptations were part of the great conflict that the Bible speaks about. Once sin entered our world in the Garden of Eden, there has been this battle between God and Satan, good and evil.

Sin was defeated on the cross by Jesus Christ. The temptations He received at the beginning of His public ministry, as well as His victory over them, set the stage for His ultimate victory on the cross. Thus, the temptation was part of this continuing struggle.

In sum, we have discovered that the temptations of Jesus took place for a number of very important reasons. Indeed, they were part of the overall plan of God for our ultimate salvation from sin.

Why Is Jesus Called The Last Adam And The Second Man?

The Bible calls Jesus both the "last Adam" and the "second Man." Paul wrote to the Corinthians with this explanation of Jesus.

> The Scriptures tell us, "The first man, Adam, became a living person." But the last Adam—that is, Christ—is a life-giving Spirit. What came first was the natural body, then the spiritual body comes later. Adam, the first man, was made from the dust of the earth, while Christ, the second man, came from heaven. Every human being has an earthly body just like Adam's, but our heavenly bodies will be just like Christ's (1 Corinthians 15:45-48 NLT).

What does this mean? In what sense was Jesus Christ called the "Last Adam" and the "Second Man?"

1. ADAM WAS THE FIRST PERFECT MAN

These two names of Jesus compare Him with Adam. Adam was the first man who was created by God. The Bible says that the God of the Bible made Adam out of the dust of the earth. We read in Genesis.

> The LORD God formed the man from the dust of the ground and breathed into his nostrils the breath of life, and the man became a living being (Genesis 2:7 NIV).

The Bible says that upon his creation Adam had one nature—that of a human. While it was a perfect human nature, he was also given choice. In other words, he had the possibility of being disobedient to God. Unfortunately, Adam did disobey God.

After the sin of Adam and Eve, animal sacrifices were brought to God. Yet the blood of animals could not take away the sin of Adam and the rest of his fallen human race. God had to have perfect human nature sacrificed in place of sinful human nature. The physical descendants of Adam would not qualify.

2. JESUS THE LAST MAN BORN WITHOUT A SIN NATURE

The Lord Jesus is the last Adam and the Second Man. He is the last man to be born without a sin nature—Adam was the first. Everyone who came after Adam and Eve were born with sinful nature. Scripture says.

> When Adam had lived 130 years, he had a son in his own likeness, in his own image; and he named him Seth (Genesis 5:3 NIV).

The likeness of Adam was a sinful likeness.

Jesus, like Adam was born without a sinful nature but in contrast to Adam, the nature of Jesus Christ, God the Son, was both human and divine.

During His public ministry Jesus made it clear that He never committed any type of sin. Indeed, He asked the following question to the people of His day.

> Which of you convicts Me of sin? And if I tell the truth, why do you not believe Me? (John 8:46 NKJV).

Nobody had seen Him sin. No one could convict Him of sin because Jesus never sinned.

3. JESUS WAS THE MAN FROM HEAVEN

He was the "Second Man"—the man from heaven. In contrast, Adam the first man was created from the dust of the ground.

As the God-man, Jesus could be the suitable sacrifice for the sins of the world. The Bible says that Jesus offered Himself as the sacrifice for sin. Paul wrote the following to the Corinthians.

> This means that anyone who belongs to Christ has become a new person. The old life is gone; a new life has begun! And all of this is a gift from God, who brought us back to himself through Christ. And God has given us this task of reconciling people to him. For God was in Christ, reconciling the world to himself, no longer counting people's sins against them. And he gave us this wonderful message of reconciliation. So we are Christ's ambassadors; God is making his appeal through us. We speak for Christ when we plead, "Come back to God!" For God made Christ, who never sinned, to be the offering for our sin, so that we could be made right with God through Christ (2 Corinthians 5:17-21 NLT).

As the second man, the man from heaven, Jesus could be the perfect sacrifice for the sins of the world. He accomplished what the rest of Adam's race could not accomplish—live a life of sinless perfection. In doing so, He was able to be the sacrifice for sin.

Therefore, Christ, like Adam was created perfect, but unlike Adam He never sinned. This allowed Him to be the perfect sacrifice for a fallen race of human beings.

SUMMARY TO QUESTION 28
WHY IS JESUS CALLED THE LAST ADAM AND THE SECOND MAN?

Two of the titles we find given to Jesus are the "Last Adam" as well as the "Second Man." It is important that we understand why He was called these things.

Adam, the first human, was created perfect. In other words, he did not have a sin nature. Jesus is the "last Adam" in the sense that He was the last man who did not have a sin nature. There will never be another person who is born without a sin nature. Jesus, however, in contrast to Adam, never sinned.

Although Jesus was like Adam, in that He did not have a sin nature, He was different from Adam in that He was from heaven. This is why He is called the "Second Man." The first man was created from the dust of the earth, while the Second Man has His origin in heaven.

Consequently, as the only One who lived a perfect life while He was here upon the earth, Jesus was able to be the sinless sacrifice for the sins of the world.

Is The Virgin Birth To
Be Understood Literally?

The Bible teaches the "Virgin Birth," or more properly, the "Virgin Conception" of Jesus Christ. Indeed, the New Testament records the fact that God the Son became a human being in the Person of Jesus Christ. The means through which this was accomplished by the Virgin Birth—Jesus was conceived without the aid of a human male. It was a miraculous birth though it was a genuine human birth.

The Bible has a number of important things to say about this matter. We must make the following observations.

1. FROM EVE TO CHRIST: ALL HUMANS WERE CONCEIVED BY NATURAL PROCESSES

When God made the first man Adam, He made his body out of the dust of the earth. We read about this in the Book of Genesis.

> The LORD God formed the man from the dust of the ground and breathed into his nostrils the breath of life, and the man became a living being (Genesis 2:7 NIV).

Adam was formed from the earth, from the dust of the ground.

On the other hand, Eve, the first woman, was created from the side of Adam. This is also described in the second chapter of Genesis.

> So the LORD God caused the man to fall into a deep sleep; and while he was sleeping, he took one of the man's ribs and closed up the place with flesh. Then the LORD God made a woman from the rib he had taken out of the man, and he brought her to the man (Genesis 2:21,22 NIV).

She, like Adam, was supernaturally created. Neither Adam nor Eve had a human father or mother.

All humans, since that time, have received their body through the natural processes, the union between a man and a woman.

2. JESUS WAS CONCEIVED WITHOUT THE AID OF A HUMAN MALE

However, when Jesus Christ was conceived, it was without the aid of a human male. We read of the angel Gabriel explaining to Mary the conception of the Christ Child.

> And Mary said to the angel, "How will this be, since I am a virgin. And the angel answered her, "The Holy Spirit will come upon you, and the power of the Most High will overshadow you; therefore the child to be born will be called holy— the Son of God (Luke 1:34-35 ESV).

According to Scripture, Jesus' birth was miraculous. Indeed, it was one- of-a-kind. Nobody, before or since, has entered our world in this particular manner.

3. THE OLD TESTAMENT PREPARATION FOR THE VIRGIN BIRTH

The Virgin Birth, or Virgin Conception, had been part of the plan of the God of the Bible from the very beginning. Indeed, it was prefigured in the Old Testament.

In Genesis 3:15, we read of God announcing the following judgment to the serpent in the Garden of Eden after the sin of Adam and Eve.

I will put enmity between you and the woman, and between your offspring and her offspring; he shall bruise your head, and you shall bruise his heel (Genesis 3:15 ESV).

The Contemporary English Version puts it this way.

You and this woman will hate each other; your descendants and hers will always be enemies. One of hers will strike you on the head, and you will strike him on the heel (Genesis 3:15 CEV).

The offspring of the woman is a prediction of the coming Messiah—the Deliverer. This is where this prediction will find its ultimate fulfillment. In other words, the Messiah was to be born from the "offspring of the woman."

The offspring of the woman would bruise the head of the offspring of the serpent. The promise gives the first hint of the Virgin Birth. We can make some further observations.

A. THE MESSIAH WOULD BE VIRGIN BORN

As the Old Testament history began to unfold, further evidence was given that the Messiah would be virgin born. We read the following predictions in the Book of Isaiah.

The Lord himself will choose the sign. Look! The virgin will conceive a child! She will give birth to a son and will call him Immanuel—'God is with us' (Isaiah 7:14 NLT).

There has been considerable controversy about the Hebrew word almah, used in Isaiah 7:14, whether it means "virgin" or "young woman." In fact, many English translations use "young woman" instead of virgin when translating this verse.

For example, we read the following in the New English Translation.

> For this reason the sovereign master himself will give you a
> confirming sign. Look, this young woman is about to con-
> ceive and will give birth to a son. You, young woman, will
> name him Immanuel (Isaiah 7:14 NET).

The word is not a technical term for "virgin." Rather, it means a young woman who has the characteristics of virginity. However, it should be noted that in all seven occurrences of *almah* in the Old Testament it never refers to a young woman who has lost her virginity.

Supposedly there is a better term in Hebrews for virgin—*bethulah*. Yet *bethulah* is not a technical term for a virgin.

B. THE WOMAN WAS ASSUMED TO BE A VIRGIN

Even if Isaiah was only referring to a young woman who was ready for marriage, the assumption would be that she was a virgin. Under the Mosaic Law, a woman could be stoned to death for having a child out of wedlock. What can be said is that *almah* is consistent with the idea of a young woman who has not had any sexual relations with a man. In other words, she would be a virgin.

THE EVIDENCE FROM THE SEPTUAGINT TRANSLATION

There is also the issue of the Septuagint translation. The Old Testament was translated from the original Hebrew into Greek some two hundred years before the time of Christ. This translation is known as the Septuagint, or seventy. When they translated the Hebrew word almah in Isaiah 7:14, they used the Greek word *parthenos*.

This is the usual word for "virgin." Hence we can observe that before the time of Christ, it seemed that the people understood the passage to refer to a special birth. However, it is probably too much to say that the people were expecting the Messiah to be virgin born.

4. THE NEW TESTAMENT EVIDENCE

While the virgin birth is predicted, as well as implied in the Old Testament, the New Testament writers make it clear that Jesus Christ was virgin born. The evidence is as follows.

MATTHEW

The Gospel of Matthew makes it clear that Jesus was miraculously conceived. On a number of occasions, Matthew relates the supernatural way in which Jesus came into the world.

A. THE LISTING IN JESUS' GENEALOGY

In Matthew 1:2-15 we have a number of people listed who fathered children. For example, it says, "Abraham begat, or fathered, Isaac." Each name in the genealogy is written this way.

However, in verse 16 there is a change in the way in which the genealogy is written. Rather than saying that someone "fathered" the son, the phrase reads, "Jesus was born." Nothing is said about Joseph being the father of Jesus.

In contrast to all the preceding people listed in the genealogy, Joseph is not said to have fathered Jesus but rather Jesus was born to Mary. This deliberate change of phrasing emphasizes that Joseph had nothing to do with the conception of Jesus.

B. THE CHRIST IS BORN OF MARY NOT JOSEPH

Matthew is always careful to state that Jesus was born of Mary, not Joseph. He writes.

> Jacob [was] the father of Joseph the husband of Mary, of whom Jesus was born, who is called the Messiah (Matthew 1:16 NRSV).

The phrase "of whom" is in the feminine gender in Greek. Consequently, it cannot refer to Joseph but must refer to Mary! The New Living Translation puts it this way.

> Jacob was the father of Joseph, the husband of Mary. Mary was the mother of Jesus, who is called the Messiah (Matthew 1:16 NLT).

Jesus was Mary's child, not Joseph's. The New Testament always makes this abundantly clear.

C. THE HOLY SPIRIT IS THE SOURCE JESUS' BIRTH

On two occasions, Matthew makes it plain that the Holy Spirit was the source of Jesus' conception. We read the following in the first chapter.

> Now the birth of Jesus Christ was as follows: After His mother Mary was betrothed to Joseph, before they came together, she was found with child of the Holy Spirit. Then Joseph her husband, being a just man, and not wanting to make her a public example, was minded to put her away secretly. But while he thought about these things, behold, an angel of the Lord appeared to him in a dream, saying, "Joseph, son of David, do not be afraid to take to you Mary your wife, for that which is conceived in her is of the Holy Spirit" (Matthew 1:18-20 NKJV).

Matthew makes it unambiguous to his readers that Jesus was not the physical son of Joseph. Jesus was supernaturally conceived.

D. THE FULFILLED PROPHECY OF ISAIAH

Matthew also cited Isaiah 7:14 in identifying Jesus as the fulfillment of Isaiah's prophecy of a virgin birth.

> So the Lord's promise came true, just as the prophet had said, "A virgin will have a baby boy, and he will be called

Immanuel," which means "God is with us" (Matthew 1:22,23 CEV).

He understood the prophecy to predict that the Messiah would be virgin born.

There is something else which must be appreciated. Matthew was one of the original twelve apostles. Therefore, it is possible that the virgin birth of Christ was part of what the apostles taught the first church at Jerusalem. We are told.

> All the believers devoted themselves to the apostles' teaching, and to fellowship, and to sharing in meals (including the Lord's Supper), and to prayer (Acts 2:42 NLT).

It is quite possible that the teaching of the virgin conception of Jesus was part of the apostles' teaching, or doctrine.

LUKE

Luke, the writer of the third gospel, also testified to the virgin conception of Jesus. The evidence is as follows.

A. LUKE'S TESTIMONY TO THE VIRGIN BIRTH

While Matthew was writing to a Jewish audience, Luke, a Gentile doctor, was writing to a Gentile audience. He, like Matthew, emphasized Jesus' virgin conception. Twice in his account of the annunciation of Jesus' conception, he refers to Mary as a virgin. We read.

> In the sixth month, the angel Gabriel was sent by God to a town in Galilee called Nazareth, to a virgin engaged to a man named Joseph, of the house of David. The virgin's name was Mary (Luke 1:26,27 HCSB).

Luke clearly specifies that Mary was a virgin.

Since she was a virgin, Mary asked the obvious question about how she could have a child. Luke records the following.

> Mary asked the angel, "But how can this happen? I am a virgin" (Luke 1:34 NLT).

She realized that if she were to have a child, it would be from a miraculous birth.

The angel made it clear that the conception of this child would indeed be a miracle. Luke explains what he said.

> The angel answered her, "The Holy Spirit will come to you, and the power of the Most High will overshadow you. Therefore, the holy child developing inside you will be called the Son of God" (Luke 1:35 God's Word).

The conception of the child would be miraculous. Indeed, the Holy Spirit would be the One involved in the conception of this child rather than a human male.

We also find that the child will be called "the Son of God Most High." The angel said.

> He will be great and will be called the Son of God Most High. The Lord God will make him king, as his ancestor David was (Luke 1:32 CEV).

He is never called the biological son of Joseph.

B. JESUS WAS THE SON OF MARY

We note that in the announcement of the conception of Jesus, the emphasis is on the fact the He is "her Son." In the birth narrative, Jesus is never called "Joseph's son," "his Son," or "their Son." Rather, Jesus is the "Son of the Highest," and the "Son of God." Clearly Joseph was not the actual father of Jesus.

HIS FATHER WAS GOD, NOT JOSEPH

There is more. At age twelve, Jesus Himself reminded Mary who His "real Father" was. They found Jesus in the temple, confounding the elders with His wisdom. The Bible then explains what occurred.

So when they saw Him, they were amazed; and His mother said to Him, "Son, why have You done this to us? Look, Your father and I have sought You anxiously." And He said to them, "Why did you seek Me? Did you not know that I must be about My Father's business?" (Luke 2:48,49 NKJV).

His Father was God—not Joseph. Jesus had to be about His business.

Later, in Jesus' genealogy, Luke identified Him as follows.

When Jesus began to preach, he was about thirty years old. Everyone thought he was the son of Joseph (Luke 3:23 CEV).

While people may have assumed Jesus was Joseph's son, in reality, He had no human father.

LUKE RECEIVED THESE TRUTHS FROM EYEWITNESSES

It is important to note that Luke's gospel is based upon his careful research as a historian. He explained this in his prologue.

Many people have tried to tell the story of what God has done among us. They wrote what we had been told by the ones who were there in the beginning and saw what happened. So I made a careful study of everything and then decided to write and tell you exactly what took place. Honorable Theophilus, I have done this to let you know the truth about what you have heard (Luke 1:1-4 CEV).

The virgin birth of Christ was not just a rumor or a myth. Indeed, it was the actual way in which God the Son entered into this word. While it is not a miracle that can be verified by eyewitnesses, such as the resurrection, we have the testimony of Mary and Joseph.

JESUS' TEACHING ON HIS ORIGIN: HE WAS FROM ABOVE

Jesus Himself taught that His origin was from above.

> Jesus said to them, "You're from below. I'm from above. You're from this world. I'm not from this world" (John 8:23 God's Word)

This statement is about as clear as you can get.

John also records Him saying the following.

> Jesus replied, "If God were your Father, you would love me, for I have come from God and am now here. I have not come on my own initiative, but he sent me (John 8:42 NET).

Jesus said that He had come from God. He realized that His birth was miraculous.

JESUS ACKNOWLEDGED MARY AS HIS MOTHER

Jesus also acknowledged Mary as His mother. We also read about this in the Gospel of John. He wrote.

> When Jesus saw His mother and the disciple He loved standing there, He said to His mother, "Woman, here is your son" (John 19:26 HCSB).

He never said that Joseph was His father. Never.

Others spoke of Jesus as the "son of Joseph." We read of this in Luke's account.

> All were speaking well of him, and were amazed at the gracious words coming out of his mouth. They said, "Isn't this Joseph's son" (Luke 4:22 NET).

However, the Bible is clear that Jesus was not the physical son of Joseph. He only could be called Joseph's son in the adopted sense.

JESUS CLAIMED GOD AS HIS FATHER

While at age twelve, Jesus reminded His mother Mary that God was His Father, He also claimed God as His Father when He was an adult.

In fact, on a number of occasions during His public ministry, Jesus claimed that God was His Father. When Jesus cleansed the temple He said.

> To those who sold the doves he said, "Take these things away from here! Do not make my Father's house a marketplace" (John 2:16 NET).

This was "His Father's house." It was not "their father's house."

JESUS CLAIMED EQUALITY WITH THE FATHER

Later, Jesus claimed equality with God the Father. In the Gospel of John, we read of this astounding claim of the Lord.

> But Jesus said, "My Father has never stopped working, and that is why I keep on working." Now the leaders wanted to kill Jesus for two reasons. First, he had broken the law of the Sabbath. But even worse, he had said that God was his Father, which made him equal with God (John 5:17,18 CEV).

Jesus clearly claimed that God was His Father, not Joseph. This is one of the reasons why the Jewish leadership wanted to kill Christ. They understood what He was claiming. To them, it was blasphemy.

THE TESTIMONY OF GOD THE FATHER

God the Father also testified that Jesus Christ was His Son. The New Testament records three different occasions in which the Father acknowledged the Son with an audible voice.

THE FATHER ACKNOWLEDGED JESUS AT HIS BAPTISM

At Jesus' baptism, we read about God the Father giving testimony to the identity of the One who was baptized.

> And when Jesus was baptized, immediately he went up from the water, and behold, the heavens were opened to him, and he saw the Spirit of God descending like a dove and coming to rest on him; and behold, a voice from heaven said, "This is my beloved Son, with whom I am well pleased" (Matthew 3:16-17 ESV).

On this occasion, the Father verbally acknowledged Jesus as His Son.

THE FATHER ACKNOWLEDGED JESUS AT THE TRANSFIGURATION

At the Transfiguration of Jesus, the Father again testified to the Son. Matthew wrote.

> While he was still speaking, suddenly a bright cloud covered them, and a voice from the cloud said: This is My beloved Son. I take delight in Him. Listen to Him! (Matthew 17:5 HCSB).

Therefore, we have a further confirmation of Jesus' claims by God the Father.

THE FATHER ACKNOWLEDGED JESUS IN FRONT OF THE CROWDS

Finally, in front of the multitudes, the Father again recognized the Son. We read the following statement of Jesus in the Gospel of John.

> Now I am deeply troubled, and I don't know what to say. But I must not ask my Father to keep me from this time of suffering. In fact, I came into the world to suffer. So Father, bring glory to yourself. A voice from heaven then said, "I have already brought glory to myself, and I will do it again!" (John 12:27,28 CEV).

In doing this, the Father acknowledged Jesus as His Son with an audible voice in front of the large crowds.

IT WAS AN APPROPRIATE ENTRANCE INTO THE WORLD FOR GOD'S SON

The virgin birth was an appropriate entrance of God the Son, Jesus Christ, into the world. Since He lived a miraculous life, that finished with the miracle of His resurrection and ascension, it is not inconsistent that He would enter the world with a miraculous birth. Therefore, the virgin birth is in complete harmony with the other miraculous elements of the life of Jesus.

SUMMARY TO QUESTION 29
IS THE VIRGIN BIRTH TO BE UNDERSTOOD LITERALLY?

The evidence is clear that God the Son, Jesus Christ, came into the world by means of a virgin birth, or virgin conception. While God directly created the man Adam, the first woman, Eve, was taken from the body of Adam.

All humans since then have received their body through the union of a man and a woman. Jesus Christ was different. He entered the world without the aid of a human male. It was at the same time a miraculous conception and a human birth. This can be seen as follows.

The Old Testament predicted the virgin birth of the coming Messiah. It started in the Garden of Eden and then continued throughout the Old Testament period. While it was not a major emphasis in the teachings of the Hebrew Scriptures, we do find it there.

It is the New Testament where we find the doctrine of the virgin birth or virgin conception, more fully revealed. Matthew and Luke record the fulfillment of the promise. Each of these New Testament writers identifies Mary as a virgin.

In his genealogy, Matthew makes it clear that Jesus was not the physical son of Joseph. He then went on to say that Mary was pregnant before she and Joseph had any type of physical relationship.

Matthew records the angel of the Lord visiting Joseph who announced that Mary's pregnancy was a supernatural work of God. The remainder of Matthew's gospel consistently teaches that Jesus was supernaturally conceived.

Luke's gospel teaches the same thing. He records the conversation the angel Gabriel had with Mary when she was still a virgin. From this episode, it is clear that the conception of the child was supernatural. As is true with Matthew, Luke consistently emphasizes that Jesus' conception was a miraculous work of God.

During His public ministry, Jesus Himself testified to the fact that God was His Father. He too acknowledged that He had a miraculous conception. Never do we find Jesus teaching that Joseph was His "biological Father."

We also find that God the Father verbally acknowledge Jesus as His "unique Son" on three different occasions. At Jesus' baptism, His transfiguration, as well as on one occasion in front of the crowds, the Father audibly testified to the Son.

Consequently, the virgin birth, or more properly, the virgin conception of Jesus Christ, is an established truth of the New Testament.

Why Do We Find The Virgin Birth Only Recorded In Matthew And Luke?

The virgin birth, or the virgin conception, of Jesus Christ is only recorded in two of the four gospels—Matthew and Luke. Mark and John do not mention it at all. The remainder of the New Testament says nothing specifically about it. If it is such an important belief, then why don't we find it recorded in the Book of Acts, and the writings of Paul?

Some have argued that two of the Gospel writers, Mark and John, as well as the Apostle Paul, do not record the Virgin Birth because they knew nothing of it. However, this argument is unconvincing for the following reasons.

EACH WRITER ADDRESSED A PARTICULAR AUDIENCE

To begin with, we must realize that each Gospel writer addresses his work to a particular audience and, in doing so, records a different aspect of the life of Christ.

MARK

Mark is emphasizing that Jesus is the servant of the Lord, and that He can miraculously perform the job God ordained Him to do. Mark says nothing about the first thirty years of the life of Christ. The reason that nothing is said in regard to Jesus' birth, or early years, is that it is not relevant to Mark's purpose. We should not assume that he was unaware of what took place.

JOHN

The same is true with the gospel of John. John emphasizes that Jesus was God from all eternity. In fact, the gospel begins in eternity past with Jesus already on the scene. John then stresses the fact that Jesus, as God, became a human.

> So the Word became human and lived here on earth among us. He was full of unfailing love and faithfulness. And we have seen his glory, the glory of the only Son of the Father (John 1:14 NLT).

Consequently, John is emphasizing the sublime truth that God came into the world—not the manner in which He came. He says nothing about Jesus' first thirty years. Again, this was not his purpose in writing the gospel.

JOHN RECORDS PHILIP CALLING HIM JESUS OF NAZARETH

In John's gospel, we find Philip calling Jesus, "Jesus of Nazareth, the son of Joseph." The account reads as follows.

> Philip then found Nathanael and said, "We have found the one that Moses and the Prophets wrote about. He is Jesus, the son of Joseph from Nazareth" (John 1:45 CEV).

However, this is irrelevant to the question of the virgin birth of Jesus—since John has already told his readers that Jesus existed in the beginning as God.

THEY DO NOT DENY IT

Though the writers Mark and John do not expressly state that Jesus was born of a virgin, nowhere do they teach the contrary. We do not find

Joseph ever spoken of as Jesus' Father by either of these writers. They simply give us no details concerning His birth, or who was His Father.

IT IS AN ARGUMENT FROM SILENCE

The argument that Mark and John did not know about the virgin conception of Jesus is an argument from silence. At best, an argument from silence is usually not a very strong reason to believe something. Because someone does not state a fact, it does not necessarily follow that the person was unaware of that particular fact. It may mean the person, for whatever reason, chose not to mention it. Indeed, this is exactly what we have in this case.

THESE TWO GOSPELS IMPLY THE KNOWLEDGE OF A VIRGIN BIRTH

There is something else. The Gospels of Mark and John imply knowledge of the virgin birth without expressly stating it.

A. THE TESTIMONY OF MARK

In Luke's gospel, Jesus is called the son of Joseph by the crowds. We read.

> All the people started talking about Jesus and were amazed at the wonderful things he said. They kept on asking, "Isn't he Joseph's son?" (Luke 4:22 CEV).

Because Luke has already told his readers that Jesus was born of a virgin they understand when people call Jesus the "son of Joseph" in ignorance. Luke was merely reporting their assumptions as to Jesus' parentage.

On the other hand, Mark is careful not to use that phrase. In Mark, Jesus is called the "son of Mary." We read.

> Isn't this the carpenter, the son of Mary, and the brother of James, Joseph, Judas, and Simon? Aren't his sisters here with us? So they took offense at him (Mark 6:3 HCSB).

Consequently, Mark makes the point that Jesus is Mary's son but says nothing about Joseph being the father of Jesus. Therefore, he says nothing that would contradict the idea of a virgin birth, or a virgin conception.

B. THE TESTIMONY OF JOHN

In John's gospel, Jesus' divine origin had been a cause for argumentation with the religious leaders. He told them that His origin was from heaven.

> I speak what I have seen in the presence of the Father, and therefore you do what you have heard from your father (John 8:38 HCSB).

As a further demonstration of His divine authority, Jesus emphasizes His heavenly origin to these doubting religious leaders.

The Jews responded to this saying that Abraham was their father. Then they made the following accusation at Jesus.

> You are doing the works your father did." They said to him, "We were not born of sexual immorality. We have one Father—even God." (John 8:41 ESV).

Note that they accused Him of being an illegitimate child. This shows they were aware of the fact that Mary had become pregnant before her marriage to Joseph. This gives further credence to the account of the virgin birth as recorded by Matthew, which states that Joseph considered divorcing her privately when he had discovered her pregnancy.

In recording this dialogue between Jesus and the religious leaders, John implies that the birth of Jesus was not ordinary but came through unusual circumstances. As Matthew and Luke so clearly tell us, it was not Mary's unfaithfulness that made it an unusual birth, but rather the fact that the God of the Bible had performed a miracle having Jesus conceived not by a man, but by the Holy Spirit.

Therefore, while these gospel writers do not explicitly say that Jesus was born of a virgin, we have their implied testimony to His virgin conception.

THE TESTIMONY OF THE APOSTLE PAUL

The fact that the Apostle Paul does not record the virgin conception is not surprising. In his various letters, he does not deal with the story of the earthly life of Jesus Christ whatsoever. This is not his emphasis or his purpose. However, he does say the following about Jesus.

> But when the time was right, God sent his Son, and a woman gave birth to him. His Son obeyed the Law (Galatians 4:4 CEV).

Certainly this means more than Jesus had a mother. It could suggest that he had only a human mother but not a human father. However, it is also possible that Paul simply meant that Jesus, God the Son, became a genuine human being.

In sum, we find that Mark, John and Paul cannot be used as witnesses against the virgin conception of Jesus. While not explicitly stated in their gospels, or in Paul's letters, the virgin conception is certainly consistent with everything else which they teach about Jesus.

SUMMARY TO QUESTION 30
WHY DO WE FIND THE VIRGIN BIRTH ONLY RECORDED IN MATTHEW AND LUKE?

The virgin birth, or virgin conception, of Jesus Christ is clearly recorded in two of the four gospels—Matthew and Luke. These two writers make it plain that God the Son came into our world through the means of a miraculous conception. There is no doubt that each of them expressly taught this.

The other two gospels, Mark and John say nothing specifically about it. This has caused some people to argue that they did not know of the teaching—or that they knew of it, but did not believe it.

Yet the evidence does not lead us to these conclusions. Mark is careful to call Jesus "the Son of Mary" but not the "Son of Joseph." Furthermore, there is nothing in his gospel which teaches anything contrary to the virgin conception of Christ. It was not his purpose to deal with this issue. Indeed, Mark says nothing about Jesus' early years.

John emphasizes that God became a human being in the Person of Jesus Christ. He is not interested in giving us any details of Jesus' birth—or anything about His life before He began His public ministry. John does, however, indicate that there was a controversy over the exact identification of Jesus' Father. Thus, he gives evidence of his knowledge of the virgin conception.

The Apostle Paul says nothing of the virgin birth because he does not deal with the earthly life of Christ. His purpose was to explain the meaning of the death and resurrection of the Lord rather than dealing with how He entered our world. Like Mark and John, the virgin conception was not a matter of emphasis in his writings.

Consequently, the fact that some New Testament writers do not mention the virgin conception of Jesus Christ does not in any way prove they rejected the doctrine, or knew nothing of it.

Why Is The Doctrine Of The Virgin Birth Important?

The Bible teaches the virgin birth, or the virgin conception of Jesus Christ. Christians have considered it as one of the essentials doctrines of the faith. The question before us is simple: Why is this one doctrine so important? Does it really matter whether or not Jesus was born of a virgin?

Yes, indeed it does. There are at least five reasons why it is important to believe in the virgin birth, the virgin conception. They are as follows.

1. JESUS HAD A HEAVENLY ORIGIN

The most important reason to hold the belief in the virgin conception concerns Jesus' identity as God the Son, the Second Person of the Holy Trinity.

If Joseph were His true father, then Jesus would be only a human being. He would not be the Son of God as Scripture clearly states. He would have had His beginning in time rather than eternally existing.

The Bible, however, states that God the Son, who became the Man Jesus Christ, had no beginning. John's gospel states it this way.

> In the beginning was the Word, and the Word was with God, and the Word was God (John 1:1 KJV).

Thus, the virgin birth is crucial to Jesus being the Son of God.

2. JESUS HAD A SINLESS NATURE

A second reason why the virgin birth is important concerns the sinless character of Christ. If Jesus had a human father, then seemingly He would have inherited a sinful nature as the rest of us have. The Bible says.

> Therefore, just as sin came into the world through one man, and death through sin, and so death spread to all men because all sinned (Romans 5:12 ESV).

Scripture possibly teaches that the sin nature is passed through by male rather than the female. If this is the case, then Jesus would have inherited a sin nature had He had a human father.

Yet the Scripture states that Jesus Christ never sinned. In summing up the life of Jesus, Peter wrote the following about Him.

> He committed no sin, neither was deceit found in his mouth (1 Peter 2:22 ESV).

Clearly, the New Testament writers thought that He was sinless.

John the Apostle also testified that Jesus was without sin. We read these words from him.

> You know that he appeared in order to take away sins, and in him there is no sin (1 John 3:5 ESV).

Again we have the emphasis that in Jesus there is no sin. However, if Jesus were the actual son of Joseph, then His sinless character would only be a myth.

3. JESUS WAS THE PERFECT SACRIFICE

A third reason why the virgin birth is crucial to the Christian faith concerns our salvation from sin. Without the sinlessness of Jesus Christ, there would be no salvation for us. To be the perfect sacrifice, Jesus had to be unblemished. In other words, He had to be without sin.

HE CAME TO SET PEOPLE FREE FROM SIN

According to the Apostle Paul, God the Son, Jesus Christ, came into our world to save those who were under the law. He wrote the following to the Galatians.

> But when the time was right, God sent his Son, and a woman gave birth to him. His Son obeyed the Law so he could set us free from the Law, and we could become God's children (Galatians 4:4,5 CEV)

The Son of God came into the world at the fullness of time. In doing so, He was able to set people free from the bondage of the Law by being our sacrifice for sin.

This echoes Jesus' own statement as to the purpose of His coming into the world. Luke records Jesus saying the following.

> And I, the Son of Man, have come to seek and save those like him who are lost (Luke 19:10 NLT).

Jesus came to be our Savior.

In doing so, He had to be the unblemished Lamb of God. Indeed, God required a sacrifice that was without blemish. We read of this in Exodus.

> Your lamb shall be without blemish, a male a year old (Exodus 12:5 ESV).

If Jesus were a sinner in any sense of the word, then He could not provide salvation for us. However, because He came into the world by supernatural means and lived a sinless life, Christ could be that sacrifice for our sins—without spot and without blemish. The Bible makes this clear.

For God made Christ, who never sinned, to be the offering for our sin, so that we could be made right with God through Christ (2 Corinthians 5:21 NLT).

Jesus was without sin. Therefore, He qualified as the perfect sacrifice.

4. IT SHOWS THE UNIQUENESS OF CHRIST

There is something else about the virgin conception of Christ that is important. Among other things, it shows the uniqueness of Jesus Christ. No one else has ever come into the world in the same way as Jesus. The unique and miraculous nature of Jesus Christ carried on through His entire life. His birth was a miracle, His public ministry consisted of miracles, Jesus miraculously lived a sinless life, He miraculously came back from the dead, and then He left this world in a miraculous way. Consequently, from His entrance into this world until His departure, the life of Jesus Christ was a miracle. Thus, His life was certainly one-of-a-kind.

5. THE BIBLE SAYS SO

The fifth reason to believe in the virgin birth of Jesus Christ is because the Bible says so. If Jesus were not actually born of a virgin, then the Bible is wrong. If it is wrong concerning the virgin birth, then it is possible that it may be in error about other matters.

Indeed, once the door opens to the possibility of error in Scripture, then the eventual and logical result is that the entire foundation of the Christian faith will crumble. The doctrine of the virgin birth, and the credibility of Christianity, go hand-in-hand.

This sums up why the doctrine of the virgin conception of Jesus Christ is so crucial to the truthfulness of the Christian faith. Indeed, without it, there is no Christian faith.

SUMMARY TO QUESTION 31
WHY IS THE DOCTRINE OF THE VIRGIN BIRTH IMPORTANT?

One of the key doctrines in Christianity is the virgin birth or more properly, the virgin conception of Jesus Christ. There are at least five reasons why this is so. We can list them as follows.

First, it confirms Jesus' heavenly origin. According to the New Testament, He was not from this world. The fact that He did not have a human father shows the difference between Himself and all of the rest of us. He is from above—while we are from this earth. Therefore, the virgin conception highlights His heavenly origin.

Second, it is important for Jesus' sinless nature. It is possible, but not certain, that the sin nature is passed along to each of us at conception. If the sin nature is passed on by conception, then Jesus Christ, God the Son, could not have been conceived in the same manner as everyone else. Consequently, it was necessary that He had a human mother but not a human father.

Thirdly, the virgin conception was also necessary for Him to be the perfect sacrifice for our sin. Indeed, He had to be one without any defect. To be an acceptable sacrifice for our sins, Jesus had to be the unblemished "Lamb of God." This is who the Bible says that He was. Indeed, at the annunciation of His conception, He was called the "Holy, Son of God." Therefore, our eternal salvation depends upon His sinlessness.

The virgin conception also points out the uniqueness of Jesus Christ. Indeed, nobody else in the history of our planet has ever come into our world in this manner. In addition, nobody in the future will ever be born of a virgin in the same way as Jesus. He is thus one-of-a-kind.

Finally, the virgin birth is important because the Bible says that this is what happened. The authority of the Bible is at stake in this issue. If the Scripture says it happened, then it happened. The ultimate author behind the Bible, God Himself, does not lie.

These five points illustrate the importance of the virgin conception of Christ. Indeed, it is a crucial doctrine of the Christian faith.

QUESTION 32

Was The Virgin Conception Necessary?

The virgin birth is an important doctrine. This is because the Bible teaches that this is the way that God the Son became human. However, there is a related question, "Was the virgin birth necessary?" Some argue that is was absolutely necessary. Others point out that there are a number of ways that God the Son could have come into the world apart from the virgin birth. They include the following.

1. HE COULD HAVE COME TO EARTH FULLY GROWN

There is the possibility that Jesus could have come to earth as a grown man. However, if God the Father had decided to send Jesus to earth in this manner, He would not have predicted in the Old Testament that the Messiah would have been from David's family. If this had happened, He would not have had any human parents.

Consequently, He would have bypassed all the experiences that humans have until adulthood. Therefore, He could not really identify with humanity. While it is theoretically possible Jesus could have come to earth in this manner, it would not have allowed Him to experience humanity as the rest of us. For all intents and purposes this does not seem to be a real option.

2. HE COULD HAVE COME AS A RESULT OF NORMAL CONCEPTION

There is also the argument that Jesus could have come about through normal conceptions. This assumes that Jesus could have been sinless without being conceived by a virgin. Those who argue this way say that the Bible never clearly states that sin is transferred merely by conception. Therefore, Joseph could have been the actual father of Jesus without passing along a sin nature to Jesus.

Yet, if this were the case, then some sort of miracle would have had to have occurred from keeping Jesus from inheriting a sinful nature like the rest of us. Hence, some miracle was necessary for Christ to born into our world with a sinless nature.

Whatever the case may be, we know that the God the Father decided to send Jesus into the world by means of a virgin conception. Indeed, Scripture is clear that Joseph was not His biological father.

Therefore, any speculation about how God may have accomplished it some other way is really a waste of time. The virgin conception is the way in which God the Father chose to bring God the Son to us.

SUMMARY TO QUESTION 32
WAS THE VIRGIN CONCEPTION NECESSARY?

Some have argued that the virgin birth, while true, was not absolutely necessary. It is claimed that God the Son could have entered into our world in one of two other ways.

It is argued that God could have sent Jesus into the world as a grown man. This would bypass the need for the virgin conception.

However, if this were the case, then the Lord would not have specified the genealogy or family line of the Messiah in a number of Old Testament predictions. Indeed, people such as Abraham, Isaac, Jacob and David were promised that the Messiah would be one of their physical descendants. If Jesus entered as a grown man, then none of these predictions would have taken place.

Furthermore, if Jesus did enter into the world as a grown man He would not have been able to personally identify with each of us who have to go through the process of growing up. Consequently, there would be many human experiences with which He could not sympathize with us.

In addition, the Bible seems to teach that our sin nature is passed on through conception. While this is not specifically taught, it does seem to be inferred. Even if this is not how the sin nature is transferred to each of us, it would still have been necessary for some miracle to take place to bring Jesus into our world as a sinless human being.

However, there is really not much to gain from speculating as to the different ways in which God might have sent Jesus into the world. The Scripture is clear. Jesus was conceived in a supernatural way without the aid of a human father.

QUESTION 33

How Could A Virgin Birth Be Possible?

Granting that the Scriptures teach the virgin birth, or the virgin conception of Jesus Christ, the question always comes up as to how such an event could be possible. How could a virgin conceive a child in the first century A.D.? From the Bible we can make the following observations.

1. THE DETAILS OF JESUS' CONCEPTION ARE NOT STATED

It must be stated that the intricate details of how God worked within the body of Mary are not given to us. What is revealed is that the virgin birth, of virgin conception, was a supernatural act of God. The Bible says.

> Mary asked the angel, "But how can I have a baby? I am a virgin." The angel replied, "The Holy Spirit will come upon you, and the power of the Most High will overshadow you. So the baby born to you will be holy, and he will be called the Son of God" (Luke 1:34,35 NLT).

Beyond this, the Scripture is silent. Consequently, we too should be silent.

2. MARY IS PASSIVE IN THE MATTER

We learn something else. Mary was entirely passive in the matter of the virgin birth. The Bible says that Mary did not cooperate in any way in the process that brought about Jesus Christ into our world. She merely obeyed the angel Gabriel—who told her what was going to occur. It was entirely a supernatural work of God.

3. NOTHING IS IMPOSSIBLE WITH GOD

The angel Gabriel, when he made the announcement of the conception of Jesus, told Mary that nothing is impossible with God. He said.

For with God nothing shall be impossible (Luke 1:37 KJV).

Therefore, we should not concern ourselves about how God accomplished this miracle. Indeed, God can do anything that He so desires.

4. IT WAS A SUPERNATURAL ACT

One of the reasons the people deny the virgin birth of Jesus is because of its supernatural character. The Scripture, however, makes no apology for teaching the virgin birth. It is a miracle. But it is no more or less miraculous than other events the Bible records.

Therefore, it is inconsistent to accept some of the miracles recorded in Scripture and yet deny others. If one grants the possibility of God performing miracles, then why, it may be asked, is the virgin birth so remarkable?

5. GOD HAS THE POWER TO DO WHAT HE WISHES

The God of the Bible has the ability, or the power, to do whatever He so wishes to do.

For example, if one can accept at face value the statement of Genesis 1:1, "In the beginning God created the heavens and the earth," it is inconsistent to question His ability to perform any other miracle. Indeed, if God can speak the entire universe into existence, He certainly possesses the power to allow a virgin to conceive a child!

The God of the Bible has told humankind that He has that power. We read His words.

> I am the Lord, the God of all the peoples of the world. Is anything too hard for me (Jeremiah 32:27 NLT).

Consequently, the virgin conception of Jesus Christ is not beyond His power.

Therefore, the idea of God the Father bringing His Son into this world by means of a virgin conception is not an impossible feat—nor is it irrational to believe this is what took place. In fact, it certainly is not unreasonable when we understand the power that the God of Scripture possesses.

SUMMARY TO QUESTION 33
HOW COULD A VIRGIN BIRTH BE POSSIBLE?

Often it is asked how such a miracle as the virgin conception of Jesus Christ could be possible. Certain things need to be said to answer this question.

First, it must be recognized that the virgin birth of Christ is indeed a miracle. The Bible, however, does not tell us how it occurred—it merely states the fact that it did occur. Therefore, it is really worthless for us to speculate as to how it took place.

We do know that God worked a miracle in the body of Mary while she was entirely passive in the matter. In other words, she had absolutely nothing to do with the process. She merely accepted the fact that this is what was going to happen.

There is something we always need to remember in answering this question. To create a child from a virgin is not impossible with the God of the Bible. Indeed, He can do anything that He pleases.

Something else must be appreciated. The virgin conception of Christ should not be regarded as any more spectacular than any of the other miracles in which the Bible records. It is a miracle—but it should not be considered any more or less miraculous than Jesus walking upon water or feeding five thousand people with a few loaves and fish.

In addition, once the possibility is granted that God can do miracles, then the virgin birth of Christ must be decided upon the evidence.

Consequently, the doctrine of the virgin conception of Jesus Christ is consistent with what we know of the power of God. In sum, it is not irrational to believe in this miracle.

Why Was Jesus Called
The Son Of David?

In Scripture, we find that God had promised David, the first rightful king of Israel, that his throne would be established forever. The Bible records this promise of God as follows.

> For when you die, I will raise up one of your descendants, and I will make his kingdom strong. He is the one who will build a house—a temple—for my name. And I will establish the throne of his kingdom forever (2 Samuel 7:12-13 NLT).

One of David's descendants would rule over the nation.

THE SON OF DAVID WAS A TITLE FOR THE MESSIAH

This caused the people to long to see David's greater Son. Indeed, he would be the one who would rule forever. Therefore, the "Son of David" was a title for the promised Messiah.

In the New Testament, we discover that people recognized Jesus of Nazareth as the Son of David, the Messiah.

1. MATTHEW SAID JESUS WAS DAVID'S DESCENDANT

Matthew begins his gospel by linking Jesus to David.

Indeed, he calls Jesus the son of David in the very first sentence of his gospel. The opening reads as follows.

> The book of the generation of Jesus Christ, the son of David, the son of Abraham (Matthew 1:1 KJV).

Jesus descended from David. This means that He was from the right family line.

2. JESUS WAS BORN IN BETHLEHEM: THE CITY OF DAVID

The Scripture also makes it clear that Jesus was born in David's city, Bethlehem. Matthew records it as follows.

> Now after Jesus was born in Bethlehem of Judea in the days of Herod the king, behold, wise men from the East came to Jerusalem, saying, "Where is He who has been born King of the Jews? For we have seen His star in the East and have come to worship Him" (Matthew 2:1,2 NKJV).

Jesus was born in the exact same city that the Messiah was supposed to be born. In other words, He was born into the right family, as well as in the right city. Therefore, He had the proper credentials to be called "David's Son."

3. MANY PEOPLE CALLED JESUS THE SON OF DAVID

There were people who recognized Jesus as the "Son of David." We find that six times in the Gospel of Matthew, people called Jesus the "Son of David." The evidence is as follows.

TWO BLIND MEN RECOGNIZED JESUS' IDENTITY

Matthew notes that there were two blind men who wanted to be healed. Consequently, they followed Jesus and called out to Him for their healing. Matthew wrote.

When Jesus departed from there, two blind men followed Him, crying out and saying, "Son of David, have mercy on us!" (Matthew 9:27 NKJV).

They were asking the Son of David, the Messiah, for healing.

THE CROWD WONDERED IF JESUS COULD BE DAVID'S SON

On another occasion, after Jesus had performed a miraculous healing, the crowd wondered if Jesus could be David's Son. Matthew writes these words.

And all the multitudes were amazed and said, "Could this be the Son of David?" (Matthew 12:23 NKJV).

This miracle expressed their interest in His identity. Was Jesus the promised Messiah?

A GENTILE WOMAN USED THIS TITLE OF JESUS

A Canaanite woman who wanted her daughter healed used this title of Jesus. We read the following account.

Just then a Canaanite woman from that region came out and started shouting, "Have mercy on me, Lord, Son of David; my daughter is tormented by a demon" (Matthew 15:22 NRSV).

While this woman was a Gentile, and not a Jew, she still used the title of the Promised Jewish Messiah in addressing Jesus.

TWO BLIND MEN IN JERICHO CALLED HIM SON OF DAVID

In the town of Jericho, two blind men called out to Jesus as He was passing by their way. Matthew records what occurred in this manner.

As Jesus and the disciples left the town of Jericho, a large crowd followed behind. Two blind men were sitting beside the road. When they heard that Jesus was coming that way, they began shouting, "Lord, Son of David, have mercy on us" (Matthew 20:30 NLT).

They too were calling on Jesus as the Messiah when using the title "Son of David."

JESUS WAS CALLED THE SON OF DAVID DURING THE TRIUMPHAL ENTRY

When Jesus entered the city of Jerusalem on Palm Sunday, the people acknowledged Him as the "Son of David." We read in Matthew.

> Most of the crowd spread their garments on the road ahead of him, and others cut branches from the trees and spread them on the road. Jesus was in the center of the procession, and the people all around him were shouting, "Praise God for the Son of David! Blessings on the one who comes in the name of the Lord! Praise God in highest heaven!" (Matthew 21:9 NLT).

This response is extremely significant. Jesus rode into the city on a donkey. This particular act was something which the coming Messiah was predicted to do.

> Rejoice greatly, daughter of Zion! Shout, daughter of Jerusalem! Look! Your king is coming to you: he is legitimate and victorious, humble and riding on a donkey on a young donkey, the foal of a female donkey (Zechariah 9:9 NET).

Therefore, Jesus acted consistently with what the Scripture predicted about the Son of David.

4. JESUS ACKNOWLEDGED THAT HE WAS THE SON OF DAVID

The religious leaders were angry at the crowd for the recognition of Jesus as the Son of David. We find that Jesus, instead of rebuking them, encouraged this response. Matthew records what happened as follows.

But when the chief priests and the experts in the law saw the wonderful things he did and heard the children crying out in the temple courts, "Hosanna to the Son of David," they became indignant and said to him, "Do you hear what they are saying?" Jesus said to them, "Yes. Have you never read, Out of the mouths of children and nursing infants you have prepared praise for yourself" (Matthew 21:15,16 NET).

Again, we have the recognition of the people that Jesus was the Son of David, the promised Messiah. We also find Jesus, for the first time, publicly acknowledging this title.

THIS WAS CLEARLY A MESSIANIC TITLE

The Son of David was, therefore, a Messianic title. In fact, Jesus called this to the attention of the religious rulers. Matthew writes about a question which Jesus asked them.

"What do you think about the Christ? Whose son is he?" "The son of David," they replied. He said to them, "How is it then that David, speaking by the Spirit, calls him 'Lord'? For he says, "The Lord said to my Lord: "Sit at my right hand until I put your enemies under your feet." If then David calls him 'Lord,' how can he be his son?" No one could say a word in reply, and from that day on no one dared to ask him any more questions (Matthew 22:42-46 NIV).

In this discussion, Jesus points out to these religious rulers that the Messiah not only will be the Son of David, David also calls Him "Lord." In other words, even David recognizes that his greater Son will be superior to him.

In doing this, Jesus is claiming to be greater that King David himself. His questioning of the religious leaders caused them to become silent—as well as to not ask Him any further questions.

In sum, Jesus was indeed the promised Son of David, the Messiah of Israel. Not only did certain people acknowledge it, Jesus Himself accepted the title.

SUMMARY TO QUESTION 34
WHY WAS JESUS CALLED THE SON OF DAVID?

In the Old Testament, we find that King David was promised that one of his offspring would rule forever as King. This caused the people to look for this coming Deliverer, the Messiah. Among the other titles he would have, the Messiah would be the "Son of David."

We discover from the gospels that Jesus was called this promised "Son of David." In fact, Matthew begins his genealogy by showing that Jesus was a descendant of King David. He was born in the right family.

Furthermore, Matthew records that Jesus was born in the predicted place, the city of Bethlehem. Therefore, Jesus was born in David's family and in David's city.

There is still more. The Gospel of Matthew records that various people, on six different occasions, acknowledged Jesus as the Son of David. In other words, they were calling Him "the Messiah." This includes several blind men, the multitudes, and a Gentile woman.

In addition, on Palm Sunday, when the religious leaders wanted Jesus to rebuke the crowd for using this title of Him, Jesus rebuked them! He then went on to acknowledge that He was indeed the promised Son of David. He received the praise and worship of the people.

Jesus then pointed out to the religious rulers that the Messiah was David's Son, but that David also called Him, "Lord." Consequently, Jesus was claiming to be greater than David.

Therefore, from the evidence available, Jesus recognized that He was the promised One, the Son of David.

QUESTION 35

Was Jesus
The Messiah?

One of the major themes of the Old Testament is the coming of the
Messiah, or Deliverer. Was Jesus this promised Messiah? Did He have
the necessary credentials? What does the Bible say about this?

A number of observations need to be made.

1. THE MESSIAH WAS THE ANOINTED ONE

The Hebrew word translated "Messiah," in its verb form, literally
means, "to anoint." It refers to the process of consecrating the kings
and priests to their office by anointing their heads with oil. The noun
form of the word is used to refer to kings—"the Lord's anointed" We
find this use in Second Samuel. It says.

> Then Abishai son of Zeruiah said, "Shouldn't Shimei be
> put to death for this? He cursed the LORD's anointed"
> (2 Samuel 19:21 NIV).

The kings of Israel were the Lord's "anointed."

2. THE USE OF THE TERM IN THE OLD TESTAMENT

The term, "anointed" applied particularly to the kings of Israel who
served as the Lord's representatives. This included the first king of

Israel, Saul. David questioned an Amalekite who claimed to have killed King Saul.

> David asked him, "Why weren't you afraid to lift your hand to destroy the Lord 's anointed" (2 Samuel 1:14 NIV).

David recognized the position which Saul held. He was the Lord's anointed.

In some cases, we find that the actual anointing by the Holy Spirit followed the symbolic anointing with oil. Consequently, the person became anointed of the Lord in a real and living sense. We read in Samuel.

> Then Samuel took a flask of oil and poured it on Saul's head and kissed him, saying, "Has not the LORD anointed you leader over his inheritance?" (1 Samuel 10:1 NIV).

Samuel promised Saul that the Holy Spirit would come upon him. He said.

> The Spirit of the LORD will control you, you will prophesy with them, and you will be transformed into a different person (1 Samuel 10:6 HCSB).

The Holy Spirit was there to lead Saul.

The Scripture says that the Spirit of the Lord also came upon David when he was anointed. The Bible says.

> So as David stood there among his brothers, Samuel took the olive oil he had brought and poured it on David's head. And the Spirit of the LORD came mightily upon him from that day on. Then Samuel returned to Ramah (1 Samuel 16:13 NLT).

The Spirit came upon King David—as He had come upon King Saul.

3. THE WORD CAME TO HAVE A SPECIAL MEANING

The term "the Lord's anointed" came to have a special meaning. It referred to the anointed King who would rule in God's kingdom upon the earth. The Old Testament contains many references to this King and this kingdom, with the Messiah (or the Greek form, the "Christ") being one of the many designations for the King.

4. JESUS WAS THE PROMISED MESSIAH

In Jesus' day, the term Messiah (or Christ) became synonymous with the King who would rule. That is why we find people asking questions about the Messiah. John the Baptist was asked if he himself were the Christ, to which he replied, "No."

The people were divided over the issue of Jesus, whether or not He was the Christ. The New Testament makes it clear that Jesus claimed to be the promised Messiah, and that He had the credentials to back up that claim.

Therefore, Jesus is referred to as the Messiah, or the Christ, because that is the special designation of the promised King who would rule in God's kingdom. The title eventually became part of His name. He is now referred to as Jesus Christ. By doing so, we give testimony that Jesus is the special King—the anointed one sent from God.

THE MESSIAH WOULD BRING IN A NEW AGE

The Jews saw the Scripture speaking about two ages, this present age and the age to come. When the Messiah would come to the world, He would bring the new age. Consequently, they were looking for Him as well as the "golden age" which He would bring.

THE CLAIMS OF JESUS CHRIST TO BEING THE PROMISED MESSIAH

The Scriptures record several instances where Jesus either explicitly or implicitly stated that He was the Messiah. They are as follows.

A. MATTHEW 11:2-5

In Matthew 11, we find Jesus implying that He is the promised Messiah. We read the following account of Jesus' response to John the Baptist.

> When John, who was in prison, heard about the deeds of the Messiah, he sent his disciples to ask him, "Are you the one who is to come, or should we expect someone else?" Jesus replied, "Go back and report to John what you hear and see: The blind receive sight, the lame walk, those who have leprosy are cleansed, the deaf hear, the dead are raised, and the good news is proclaimed to the poor" (Matthew 11:2-5 NIV).

Jesus answered John's question about His identity by referring to the miraculous deeds He was performing. These were the signs that the Messiah would demonstrate when He came on the scene.

In fact, Isaiah 35:5,6 lists healing the blind, deaf and lame as the credentials of the Messiah.

> Then will the eyes of the blind be opened and the ears of the deaf unstopped. Then will the lame leap like a deer, and the mute tongue shout for joy (Isaiah 35:5,6 NIV).

Jesus went beyond that promise by healing the lepers and raising the dead. By stating this to the two messengers, He was clearly indicating that He believed Himself to be the Messiah—and had the credentials to prove it!

B. MATTHEW 16:13-17

The disciples of Jesus had seen Him perform many mighty works, healing the sick, raising the dead, and preaching that the kingdom of God has arrived. However, Jesus had never come right out and directly stated He was the Messiah. It was now time for Him to reveal clearly His true identity. Matthew records it as follows.

When Jesus came into the region of Caesarea Philippi, He asked His disciples, saying, "Who do men say that I, the Son of Man, am?" So they said, "Some say John the Baptist, some Elijah, and others Jeremiah or one of the prophets." He said to them, "But who do you say that I am?" Simon Peter answered and said, "You are the Christ, the Son of the living God." Jesus answered and said to him, "Blessed are you, Simon Bar-Jonah, for flesh and blood has not revealed this to you, but My Father who is in heaven" (Matthew 16:13-17 NKJV).

In this instance, we see Peter, speaking for the entire group, confessing Jesus as the Messiah. Instead of rebuking Peter for error, Jesus acknowledges his confession.

Jesus then told Peter that it was the heavenly Father who had revealed this truth to him. In this case, we have a clear acknowledgment on the part of Jesus that He believed Himself to be the Promised Messiah.

C. MATTHEW 26:63-65

During His trial at the house of Caiaphas the high priest, Jesus was falsely accused of many things. The trial climaxed with the high priest questioning Jesus concerning His identity.

Matthew records what transpired during this questioning.

But Jesus remained silent. Then the high priest said to him, "I demand in the name of the living God that you tell us whether you are the Messiah, the Son of God." Jesus replied, "Yes, it is as you say. And in the future you will see me, the Son of Man, sitting at God's right hand in the place of power and coming back on the clouds of heaven." Then the high priest tore his clothing to show his horror, shouting, "Blasphemy! Why do we need other witnesses? You have all heard his blasphemy" (Matthew 26:63-65 NLT).

When Jesus confessed in the affirmative that He was the Christ, the high priest accused Him of blasphemy—because He claimed to be Israel's Messiah.

We find that there were no doubts in the minds of the people present that Jesus believed Himself to be the Messiah. Because they did not believe His claim, they wanted to put Him to death. His claim was obvious to all.

CONFIRMING EVIDENCE FROM THE DEAD SEA SCROLLS

There is one further line of evidence that has recently come to light that confirms that Jesus truly believed Himself to be the Messiah. This evidence comes from a fragment from the Dead Sea Scrolls. Craig Evans explains.

> For much of the twentieth century a number of New Testament scholars assumed that Jesus possessed no messianic consciousness; that recognition of him as the Messiah was a post-Easter development. The publication of 4Q521 put that negative conclusion to rest. A fragment of this Qumran scroll anticipates the appearance of God's Messiah, who heaven and earth will obey. When this Messiah comes the downtrodden will be raised up, the injured will be healed, the dead will be raised up and the poor will hear the good news. Scholars immediately recognized the parallels with Jesus' reply to the imprisoned John the Baptist: 'Go and tell John what you hear and see: the blind receive their sight and the lame walk, lepers are cleansed and the deaf hear, and the dead are raised up, and the poor have the good news preached to them' (Matt. 11.4-5; Luke 7.22). The authenticity of the passage is doubted by almost no one: and now its messianic import is widely recognized. Did Jesus understand himself as God's anointed, as the Messiah? It seems he did (Craig Evans, *Jesus and His World: The Archaeological Evidence*, Westminster, John Knox Press, Louisville, Kentucky, 2012, p. 4).

In sum, from the totality of the evidence, there can be no doubt whatsoever that Jesus believed He was the Messiah, the Promised One, who would reveal God's truth to humankind.

SUMMARY TO QUESTION 35
WAS JESUS THE MESSIAH?

Jesus of Nazareth had a number of titles given to Him. Among them is the title "Messiah." It is important that we understand exactly what is meant by the word Messiah.

The word translated "Messiah" comes from the Hebrew word "to anoint." It was used for the anointing of the Hebrew kings. Eventually it took on a special meaning—it referred to the promised Deliverer whom the Lord would send to the people.

The Messiah is thus the "Christ," —the anointed one whom God would send into the world to set up an everlasting kingdom. He would be the King of the Jews.

When John the Baptist sent two of his disciples to ask about Jesus' identity, Christ then performed a number of miracles. He then told these disciples to go back to John and tell him what they had seen and heard. What they had seen were the signs the Messiah was to perform.

In a private meeting with His disciples, Jesus asked His them who they thought that He was. Peter confessed Jesus to be the Messiah, the Christ. Jesus acknowledged the confession of Peter. However, the public proclamation of Jesus as the Messiah would have to wait for a later time.

Eventually, on Palm Sunday, Jesus acknowledged His identity as the Messiah during His triumphal entry into Jerusalem. This was the first time that He allowed public worship of Himself as the "Anointed One."

Jesus then claimed to be the Messiah when He was on trial before the Jewish council. Under oath, He admitted His identity.

Therefore, there is no doubt that Jesus Christ believed He was the One which the Old Testament had promised would come into the world and bring in God's everlasting kingdom. This kingdom is indeed coming.

If Jesus Was The Messiah, Why Did His People Reject Him?

When Jesus, God the Son, came to earth His own people rejected Him. The Bible says the following about Jesus' rejection by the Jews.

> Even in his own land and among his own people, he was not accepted (John 1:11 NLT).

Even John the Baptist, the one who pointed Him out to the world as the Promised Messiah, later asked Jesus if He was truly the Messiah. Why did He do this do? Why do we find people questioning Jesus' identity as the Messiah?

THERE WAS NO GOOD REASON TO REJECT HIM

While there were many factors that led the Jewish people to reject Jesus as their Messiah, it can be stated simply: they did not believe in Him because they did not want to believe. It is the same reason most people throughout history have rejected Jesus as Messiah. It is not that they could not believe, it is that they *would* not believe! It is not that people need more evidence—it is that they do not act upon the evidence that they have.

REASONS FOR HIS REJECTION

We can make a couple of observations from the New Testament as to the reasons why Jesus was rejected as Messiah.

1. THE GOD-GIVEN RELIGIOUS SYSTEM DEGENERATED INTO A HUMAN-MADE SYSTEM

Originally, the entire religious system which was given to the nation of Israel, and recorded in the Old Testament, was done so to point people to Jesus Christ. While it was a God-given system, it degenerated into empty rituals. In other words, it became a human-made system of religion. The nation of Israel had established a counterfeit religious system. How did this happen?

2. THE ORAL LAW BECOMES EQUAL TO THE WRITTEN SCRIPTURE

The corruption of the system, which the Lord gave to the people, started out with the best of motives. The religious leaders of Israel wanted to preserve God's truth. Furthermore, they wanted this truth to apply to the daily lives of the people. So far, so good.

Therefore, they developed what was called the "oral law." Basically this was a collection of opinions of various Rabbis. For a long time, these opinions were thought to be too sacred to commit to writing.

At Jesus' time, this became known as "the tradition of the elders." While these were the mere opinions of the religious leaders, over time, these human opinions were given equal authority to the written Scripture. In practice, they were actually given even greater authority.

3. JESUS SPOKE OUT AGAINST THE TRADITION OF THE ELDERS

We find Jesus speaking out against such practices. When the religious leaders complained that Jesus' disciples did not ceremonially wash their hands before eating, He denounced their traditions in the strongest of terms. Matthew records what He said.

> He answered them, "And why do you disobey the commandment of God because of your tradition? For God said, 'Honor your father and mother' and 'Whoever insults his father or mother must be put to death.' But you say, 'If

someone tells his father or mother, "Whatever help you would have received from me is given to God," he does not need to honor his father.' You have nullified the word of God on account of your tradition. Hypocrites! Isaiah prophesied correctly about you when he said, 'This people honors me with their lips, but their heart is far from me, and they worship me in vain, teaching as doctrines the commandments of men'" (Matthew 15:3-9 NET).

It was against these human traditions which Jesus gave His strongest denunciations. While the people went through the motions, and gave lip-service to God, their hearts were far from Him. Indeed, it was these human-made traditions which actually canceled out, or nullified, God's Word. The example He gave in this instance was the "corban" issue.

THE RELIGIOUS LEADERS DEVISED WAYS OF GETTING AROUND GOD'S LAWS

Scripture taught that children were to honor their parents. Among other things, they were to take care of their financial and material needs when the situation called for it.

However, the religious leaders had devised a way to get around this commandment. Instead of the people giving to their parents the resources which could help them out, they could claim that the money was dedicated to the Lord.

In other words, it was set aside for God's use. Supposedly, it would be given to Him at some later time. In that way, they could keep the money rather than helping out their needy parents.

This practice was called "corban"—which is Hebrew for "a gift for God." By pronouncing something "corban" the people did not have to live up to their responsibility in assisting their needy parents. Indeed, since it was dedicated to God, it was considered too sacred to be used to support their parents. In doing so, they violated God's commandment of honoring their parents.

Therefore, the God-given system was destroyed not from without, but rather from within. Human commandments, which were given greater authority than Scripture, canceled out the Word of God. Jesus detested such human-made additions to God's truth.

Accordingly, the religious leaders at the time of Jesus had become corrupt. Their leadership was indicative of the spiritual state of the people. Though the people went through the proper rituals that God had commanded, their hearts were not in them. They were not that interested in the truth of God.

SALVATION BECAME A MATTER OF GOOD WORKS

These additions to the Word of God, as well as their emphasis of the religious leaders on keeping all of these human-made commandments, led to a second problem.

Forgiveness of sin now was seen as something which was earned by keeping this endless list of commandments. Instead of coming to God in faith, with a humble spirit and repentant heart, salvation became a system of merit, or good works. Consequently, the emphasis was upon what a person did rather than the condition of their heart toward the Lord.

Again, this contradicted what the Lord had revealed to the people. The prophet Micah wrote.

> He has told you, O man, what is good, and what the Lord really wants from you: He wants you to promote justice, to be faithful, and to live obediently before your God (Micah 6:8 NET).

The reason why the people were to keep the commandments of the Lord was lost. The emphasis became one of doing—not of the motivation behind the act.

4. THE ISSUE THAT CAUSED THE BREAK BETWEEN JESUS AND THE RELIGIOUS RULERS: THE SABBATH

The human-made traditions which were compiled by the religious leaders found their ultimate hypocrisy in the observance of the Sabbath. These rulers remembered that it was the lack of Sabbath-keeping that caused God to remove the nation from the land for the seventy-year Babylonian captivity. We read in Second Chronicles.

This took place to fulfill the Lord's message delivered through Jeremiah. The land experienced its sabbatical years; it remained desolate for seventy years, as prophesied (2 Chronicles 36:21 NET)

They were not going to make the same mistake again. However, in attempting to observe the Sabbath, the religious leaders added rules which were nonsensical. This led to a confrontation between them and Jesus.

Indeed, Jesus purposely healed on the Sabbath day. Mark explains what took place.

Then Jesus entered the synagogue again, and a man was there who had a withered hand. They watched Jesus closely to see if he would heal him on the Sabbath, so that they could accuse him. So he said to the man who had the withered hand, "Stand up among all these people." Then he said to them, "Is it lawful to do good on the Sabbath, or evil, to save a life or destroy it?" But they were silent. After looking around at them in anger, grieved by the hardness of their hearts, he said to the man, "Stretch out your hand." He stretched it out, and his hand was restored. So the Pharisees went out immediately and began plotting with the Herodians, as to how they could assassinate him (Mark 3:1-6 NET).

The plot to assassinate Jesus was based upon their human-made additions to Sabbath observance. Because Jesus did not keep *their* rules, they could not accept His claims to being the Messiah. Furthermore, because of the great number of people which were following after Him, they plotted to murder Him.

THE RELIGIOUS LEADERS WERE NOT INTERESTED IN THE TRUTH

All of this demonstrates that the religious leaders were not interested in discovering the truth of God. Indeed, they believed that they alone had the truth. In fact, the New Testament provides many such examples of the religious leaders attempting to suppress the truth of God.

A case in point is that of the raising of the man Lazarus from the dead. In the presence of the religious rulers, Jesus brought back Lazarus to life—this was after he had been dead for some four days.

One would think that such a miracle would at least make them consider believing in Jesus as the Messiah. Indeed, from their own testimony they never saw anyone do such miracles. But after discussing what to do with Jesus, they decided to kill Him. The Bible records what occurred as follows.

THEN, FROM THAT DAY ON, THEY PLOTTED TO PUT HIM TO DEATH (JOHN 11:53 NKJV).

Rather than causing belief in Jesus as the Messiah, it made them want to get rid of Him. But it was not only Jesus that they wanted to kill. Lazarus was walking around alive—a living testimony to the power and credentials of Jesus. Therefore, the religious leaders wanted to kill Lazarus also! We read about this in John's gospel. It says.

> Therefore the chief priests decided to also kill Lazarus, because he was the reason many of the Jews were deserting them and believing in Jesus (John 12:10,11 HCSB).

Lazarus was living proof of the power of Jesus. These corrupt religious leaders wanted to destroy the evidence.

THEY DID NOT WANT TO BELIEVE IN HIM

In sum, the reason Jesus was rejected as the Messiah had nothing to do with facts or evidence. The people in His day were so far away from the Lord in their hearts that they refused to believe the truth. Paul would later write about such people.

> For the wrath of God is revealed from heaven against all ungodliness and unrighteousness of people who suppress the truth by their unrighteousness (Romans 1:18 NET).

Notice that these people are spoken of as "suppressing the truth." This is something which they knowingly and willingly were doing. In other words, they are consciously making themselves ignorant with respect to God's truth.

Therefore, the rejection of Jesus as the Messiah was not so much a matter of they "could not believe," as much as it was, they "would not believe." Simply stated, they do not want to believe in Him.

SUMMARY TO QUESTION 36
IF JESUS WAS THE MESSIAH, WHY DID HIS PEOPLE REJECT HIM?

Jesus Christ came to the people of Israel and claimed to be their promised Messiah. He miraculously fulfilled the prophecies concerning the predicted One. Furthermore, He performed miracles which were to be the visible signs of the coming of the Messiah. Therefore, in every possible way, Jesus showed the people that He was the One they were waiting for.

Yet Jesus of Nazareth was rejected by His people. There are a number of reasons as to why this was so. Two stand out.

First, the hearts of the leadership were hardened to the truth. They were so corrupt, so far from the Lord in their hearts, that they were incapable of accepting the truth of God. This is how far they had degenerated.

This did not happen overnight. In fact, it started out harmless enough. At the beginning, the religious leaders wanted the people to obey the commandments of the Lord. To help them implement these commandments in their daily lives, the religious leaders began to add certain rules and regulations to the written Word of God.

These opinions of the religious teachers were passed down from generation to generation. Furthermore, new commandments were constantly being added to the older traditions. These human-made rules were eventually given greater authority than the Word of God itself. Therefore, the "tradition of the elders" became the final standard about how one should behave.

Consequently, these human-made traditions replaced the written Word of God as the final authority for the people. It was this "tradition of the elders" which Jesus denounced in the strongest of terms.

This led to a second problem—the way of salvation became perverted. Instead of the emphasis of coming to God in faith with a humble and repentant heart, the emphasis was upon what the people did. Indeed, their obedience to these human-made commandments was how they believed they received favor in the eyes of the Lord. Therefore, they kept these rules with utmost strictness. This missed the entire reason as to why God gave these commandments in the first place.

The main issue that caused the break between Jesus and the religious rulers was the Sabbath. These leaders had added on so many commandments as to how the Sabbath was to be observed that they missed the purpose for God giving it. Jesus deliberately healed on the Sabbath to confront their hypocrisy. This act of disobedience to their human-made commandments caused them to plot His assassination.

To sum up, the leaders, as well as their system, had gotten to the place where they would no longer listen to God's truth. No matter the evidence, they could not hear it.

This is illustrated for us in the gospel account of the raising of Lazarus. This man, who had been dead for four days, was miraculously brought back to life by Jesus Christ. The fact of Lazarus coming back from the dead caused many people to believe in Jesus as the Messiah.

However, the religious leaders had already rejected the idea that Jesus could be the Messiah—the One that God had promised to send to the people.

Consequently, when they saw that Lazarus had been raised, they wanted all the more to kill Jesus. But we are also told that they desired to kill Lazarus also! They wanted to get rid of the evidence.

The Apostle Paul would later write of people such as this. He said they were actively suppressing, or holding back, the truth of God. In other words, they were willingly ignorant of God's truth.

Unhappily this sums up the attitude of many people today. They do not believe in Jesus because they do not want to believe.

QUESTION 37

If Jesus Was The Messiah, Why Did His John The Baptist Have Doubts?

When God the Son, Jesus Christ, came to the earth, His own people rejected Him. In addition, even His own forerunner, John the Baptist, had his doubts.

Why would this happen—if he actually believed that Jesus was the Messiah? What caused him to ask the questions about Jesus?

We can make the following observations about this issue.

JOHN THE BAPTIST ACKNOWLEDGED JESUS AS THE MESSIAH

To begin with, John the Baptist, the forerunner of Jesus Christ, had pointed Jesus out as the Messiah. In the Gospel of John, we read the following.

> The next day, John saw Jesus coming toward him and said: Here is the Lamb of God who takes away the sin of the world! (John 1:29 CEV).

John clearly identified Jesus as the Messiah. He was the Lamb of God— the One who would take away the sin of the entire world. John knew that He was the Promised One.

JOHN THE BAPTIST QUESTIONS JESUS

Yet, we have the later account of John being put in prison by King Herod. The Baptist then sent two messengers to Jesus asking Him if He were the Christ, or if they should look for another. Luke writes about this episode.

> After Jesus had finished instructing his twelve disciples, he left and began teaching and preaching in the towns. John was in prison when he heard what Christ was doing. So John sent of his followers to ask Jesus, "Are you the one we should be looking for? Or must we wait for someone else?" (Matthew 11:1-3 CEV).

John's question was simple. Is Jesus of Nazareth truly the Christ—or is there someone else who is coming afterward.

In response to their inquiry, Jesus answered in such a way that left no doubt He was the Messiah. Luke writes.

> Jesus answered and said to them, "Go and tell John the things you have seen and heard: that the blind see, the lame walk, the lepers are cleansed, the deaf hear, the dead are raised, the poor have the gospel preached to them" (Luke 7:22 NKJV).

John certainly would have understood this message—for the signs Jesus was performing were the credentials of the Messiah. Indeed, when the Messiah was to appear, then the people would see miracles such as these.

WHY DID JOHN ASK THE QUESTION?

But why did John originally ask the question? Had he been mistaken about Jesus? Had Jesus let Him down? Had John wavered in faith?

There is a better answer than assuming John had doubts about Jesus' identity—or that he was in some sort of depression while in prison.

THE CIRCUMSTANCES OF THE NATION

The answer, as to why John would ask such a question, seems to lie in the circumstances of the nation Israel at that time. Jesus came into the world when Rome ruled the Jewish people with an iron hand.

There were many in the Holy Land who were proclaiming that the coming kingdom, which as predicted in the Old Testament, would come by means of a military overthrow.

Jesus came upon the scene and proclaimed God's kingdom was at hand. However, He also said it would belong to the meek, not the strong. The Lord also emphasized that His ministry was one of mercy, not judgment. The Bible says.

> For God did not send his Son into the world to condemn the world, but that the world should be saved through him (John 3:17 NET).

This message of Jesus was revolutionary. He told the people to go the extra mile, to turn the other cheek, to submit rather than resist. Furthermore, He had come as a Savior—not a Warrior-King.

JOHN PREDICTED THE MESSIAH WOULD JUDGE THE SINFUL PEOPLE

John the Baptist, on the other hand, proclaimed the vengeance the Messiah would bring on the unbelievers. Indeed, we find Him saying the following things to the religious leaders who came to his baptism.

> Many Pharisees and Sadducees also came to be baptized. But John said to them: You bunch of snakes! Who warned you to run from the coming judgment? Do something to show that you have really given up your sins. And don't start telling yourselves that you belong to Abraham's family. I tell you that God can turn these stones into children for Abraham. An ax is ready to cut the trees down at their roots. Any tree that doesn't produce good fruit will be chopped down and thrown into a fire (Matthew 3:7-10 CEV).

John was probably wondering how the kingdom could be established in the manner Jesus prescribed. His question contains the idea that Jesus was not going about it fast enough.

Jesus' answer indicates that the program was underway, but according to His schedule, not John's. The day of vengeance is something still awaiting the unbelievers in the future. Indeed, it would not occur at His First Coming.

It seems best, therefore, to take John's question as one concerned more with the tactics of Jesus in establishing His kingdom, rather than John questioning Jesus' identity as Messiah.

HE HAD THE WRONG EXPECTATION OF WHAT WOULD HAPPEN

There is also the matter of the type of Messiah which the people were expecting. Matthew made it clear the purpose of Jesus' coming as he recorded the words of the "angel of the Lord" to Joseph.

> She will give birth to a son, and you are to name Him Jesus, because He will save His people from their sins (Matthew 1:21 HCSB).

At His First Coming, Jesus' purpose was to save—not to condemn. Judgment will occur when He returns, not before.

In sum, we can say that John's questioning of Jesus as the Messiah seems more to do with tactics than His identity.

SUMMARY TO QUESTION 37
IF JESUS WAS THE MESSIAH, WHY DID JOHN THE BAPTIST HAVE DOUBTS?

Although John the Baptist had identified Jesus of Nazareth as the Promised Messiah, he sent two of his messengers to Jesus to ask if He were indeed the Christ. It seems that Jesus was not moving forward with establishing the kingdom like John wanted.

Jesus told the messengers that He was indeed the Messiah but not the type most people were expecting. Rather than coming into the world to overthrow the rule of Rome, Jesus came to give His life as a sacrifice for sins. In other words, He came to save, not to judge.

John was expecting immediate judgment of the sinful nation. This was not Jesus' purpose.

Therefore, the problem was one of expectation. Jesus emphasized that judgment would be delayed until the time that He returned to the earth. Judgment is indeed coming—but only in God's good timing.

Was Jesus The Prophet That Moses Predicted Would Come Into The World?

A prophet is a spokesman for God—one who relates the message of God to the people. They were usually unpopular at the time they were giving the message. The Old Testament tells us of many prophets that God raised up. They include as Elijah, Jeremiah and Isaiah.

The Old Testament, however, predicted that God would raise up one special Prophet who would be like Moses.

THE OLD TESTAMENT PREDICTED A SPECIAL PROPHET WOULD APPEAR

Moses wrote about a special prophet that was to come at some time in the future. This Prophet would have characteristics that were similar to Moses. We read the following in the Book of Deuteronomy.

> The LORD your God will raise up for you a prophet like me from among your fellow Israelites, and you must listen to that prophet. I will raise up a prophet like you from among their fellow Israelites. I will tell that prophet what to say, and he will tell the people everything I command him (Deuteronomy 18:15, 18 NIV).

This coming Prophet would have some similarities to Moses.

But at the time of Moses' death, this particular Prophet had not yet appeared. We read at the end of the Book of Deuteronomy the following words.

Since then, no prophet has risen in Israel like Moses, whom the LORD knew face to face (Deuteronomy 34:10 NIV).

The predicted Prophet was still yet to come.

THAT PARTICULAR PROPHET NEVER APPEARED

Furthermore, the Old Testament does not record that this particular Prophet ever appeared. At the time of Jesus' coming, the people were still looking for "the Prophet." The religious leaders asked John the Baptist if he was that "Prophet." We read of this in John's gospel.

"What then?" they asked him. "Are you Elijah?" "I am not," he said. "Are you the Prophet?" "No," he answered (John 1:21 HCSB).

John said that he was not the coming Prophet.

JESUS WAS RECOGNIZED AS THE PROPHET

When Jesus of Nazareth appeared on the scene, and started performing His miracles, He was recognized by many as the long-awaited Prophet who was to come into the world. We find the following response to Him as recorded in the Gospel of John.

When the people saw the sign He had done, they said, "This really is the Prophet who was to come into the world!" (John 6:14 HCSB).

The people realized the prediction of Moses of a coming Prophet had been fulfilled in Jesus. He was the long-awaited Prophet that Moses wrote of.

JESUS' TESTIMONY THAT HE WAS "THE" PROPHET

Jesus Himself testified that He was that Prophet. Indeed, He was the One who spoke the words from God the Father. We read the following in John's gospel.

Jesus answered them and said, "My doctrine is not Mine, but His who sent Me" (John 7:16 NKJV).

Here we have the claim of Jesus that He was sent from God. Furthermore, His teaching was also that of God the Father. In other words, He was a spokesman for God—a Prophet.

Jesus also predicted the people would realize that He came from the Father. In John's gospel, He made the following claim.

So Jesus said, "When you have lifted up the Son of Man, then you will know that I am he and that I do nothing on my own but speak just what the Father has taught me (John 8:28 NIV).

The realization of Jesus' identity would eventually occur.

In another place, we find Jesus saying the following about His own authority.

For I have not spoken on My own authority; but the Father who sent Me gave Me a command, what I should say and what I should speak and I know that His command is everlasting life. Therefore, whatever I speak, just as the Father has told Me, so I speak (John 12:49-50 NKJV).

The words of Jesus were the words of God the Father. Jesus was God's spokesman to the people—the Prophet.

Jesus again testified He was speaking the Father's words. We read about this later in the Gospel of John when He said.

Anyone who does not love me will not obey my teaching. These words you hear are not my own; they belong to the Father who sent me (John 14:24 NIV).

Jesus of Nazareth was indeed the long-awaited Prophet.

THE TESTIMONY OF HIS DISCIPLES: JESUS WAS THE PROPHET

After the death, resurrection and ascension of Jesus, His disciples also made it clear that Jesus was that Prophet like unto Moses. Peter said the following to a crowd which had gathered.

> Moses said: The Lord your God will raise up for you a Prophet like me from among your brothers. You must listen to Him in everything He will say to you. And it will be that everyone who will not listen to that Prophet will be completely cut off from the people (Acts 3:22,23 HCSB).

Therefore, it is the united testimony of the New Testament that Jesus was "the Prophet" that Moses said would come.

JESUS WAS GREATER THAN MOSES

One final point needs to be emphasized. Jesus Christ was greater than Moses. In fact, the Bible says that Jesus, God the Son, has been with the Father for all eternity. John wrote.

> No one has ever seen God. The One and Only Son— the One who is at the Father's side He has revealed Him (John 1:18 HCSB).

There is no real comparison between Jesus Christ and Moses. Indeed, Jesus has been face-to-face with God the Father for all eternity.

In sum, Moses was merely a man—Jesus was the eternal God who became a human being.

SUMMARY TO QUESTION 38
WAS JESUS THE PROPHET THAT MOSES PREDICTED WOULD COME INTO THE WORLD?

The Old Testament predicted that God would raise up a Prophet like Moses—the man who spoke with God face to face. This particular

Prophet did not appear during the entire Old Testament era. In the first century A.D., the people were still waiting for Him.

John the Baptist confessed he was not that long-awaited Prophet. However, it is the united claim of the New Testament that Jesus Christ was "the Prophet" predicted in the Old Testament.

The people, upon seeing Jesus' miracles, began to realize that He was indeed the predicted Prophet. Jesus Himself testified that He had come to the world to be the special spokesman for God the Father—the Prophet. There is no doubt whatsoever that He was the fulfillment of the Old Testament predictions.

Though the Prophet which would come was to be like Moses, there is really no comparison of Jesus with Moses. Indeed, while Moses spoke face-to-face with the Lord here upon the earth, God the Son has been in that relationship for all eternity.

To put it simply, Jesus was greater than Moses—for He was the one and only God who had eternally been face-to-face with God the Father.

Was Jesus A King?

The Old Testament not only looked forward to a Prophet raised up who was like Moses, it also predicted that Israel would have a "king." We read of this prediction in the Book of Deuteronomy. Moses wrote.

> When you enter the land the LORD your God is giving you and have taken possession of it and settled in it, and you say, "Let us set a king over us like all the nations around us," be sure to appoint over you the king the LORD your God chooses. He must be from among your own brothers. Do not place a foreigner over you, one who is not a brother Israelite (Deuteronomy 17:14,15 NIV).

This passage goes on to say what "the king" should, and should not, do. The type of king that was called for in this passage was never fulfilled by anyone who ruled Israel or Judah. David was the best king that Israel had, and he became the standard of comparison for later kings.

But David was far from the ideal king. Scripture records that he was both a murderer and adulterer. A number of points need to be made.

DAVID WAS PROMISED THAT ONE HIS DESCENDANTS WOULD BE KING FOREVER

David was given a promise of a king who would be his physical descendant. This man would rule over all of Israel. We read the following promise.

> For when you die, I will raise up one of your descendants, and I will make his kingdom strong. He is the one who will build a house—a temple—for my name. And I will establish the throne of his kingdom forever. I will be his father, and he will be my son. If he sins, I will use other nations to punish him. But my unfailing love will not be taken from him as I took it from Saul, whom I removed before you. Your dynasty and your kingdom will continue for all time before me, and your throne will be secure forever (2 Samuel 7:12-16 NLT).

This descendant of David would rule over a united nation forever. Indeed, it would be for "all time."

JESUS WAS THE KING OF THE JEWS

The New Testament gives the answer as to the identity of this "king." Jesus Christ is the true "King of the Jews." In the announcement of His conception, the angel Gabriel said the following to Mary about the Child who would be born.

> But the angel said to her, "Do not be afraid, Mary, you have found favor with God. You will be with child and give birth to a son, and you are to give him the name Jesus. He will be great and will be called the Son of the Most High. The Lord God will give him the throne of his father David, and he will reign over the house of Jacob forever; his kingdom will never end" (Luke 1:30-33 NIV).

The objection will be raised that Jesus never ruled as King of the Jews. Quite right. He was the genuine King but was rejected by the unbelieving people. The Bible says.

> He came to His own, and His own did not receive Him (John 1:11 NKJV).

The kingdom nevertheless, was rightfully His.

JESUS WAS EXECUTED AS A KING

The New Testament says that Jesus was executed as the "King of the Jews." We read in John's gospel about the sign that Pilate had placed over the cross of Jesus.

> And Pilate posted a sign over him that read, Jesus of Nazareth, the King of the Jews (John 19:19 NLT).

Though Pilate did not mean to honor Jesus, the sign recognized Jesus' rightful position. He was indeed the "King of the Jews."

THE NATURE OF HIS KINGDOM WAS NOT OF THIS WORLD SYSTEM

When Jesus had appeared before Pontius Pilate, He told the Roman leader the nature of His kingdom. John records what happened as follows.

> Jesus said, "My kingdom is not of this world. If it were, my servants would fight to prevent my arrest by the Jewish leaders. But now my kingdom is from another place." "You are a king, then!" said Pilate. Jesus answered, "You say that I am a king. In fact, the reason I was born and came into the world is to testify to the truth. Everyone on the side of truth listens to me (John 18:36,37 NIV).

Jesus' kingdom did not belong to this world system.

JESUS WILL BE THE KING OVER THE NATIONS AT HIS RETURN

He will return as the "King of the nations" or the "King over the nations." We read of this in the Book of Revelation.

> And they were singing the song of Moses, the servant of God, and the song of the Lamb: "Great and marvelous are your actions, Lord God Almighty. Just and true are your ways, O King of the nations" (Revelation 15:3 NLT).

Jesus will rule someday as the eternal king. In fact, all nations will honor Him.

JESUS WILL RULE IN RIGHTEOUSNESS FOREVER AND EVER

Jesus Christ's rule will be one of righteousness. The writer to the Hebrews declared this when he wrote the following.

> But to his Son he says, "Your throne, O God, endures forever and ever. Your royal power is expressed in righteousness" (Hebrews 1:8 NLT).

Righteousness will prevail when Jesus rules. What a wonderful day that will be!

In sum, we find that Jesus Christ is a "King." Indeed, there will come a day when He will rule and reign on this planet. The good news is that His kingdom will have no end!

SUMMARY TO QUESTION 39
WAS JESUS A KING?

The promise which was made to King David was that one of his descendants would rule forever as King over a united nation of Israel. As we examine the entire Old Testament period, we find that none of His descendants fulfilled this prediction.

Jesus of Nazareth is that descendant. At the announcement of His conception, the angel Gabriel told Mary that Jesus would be that promised King. However, at His First Coming, Jesus was rejected as King. Instead of ruling over the nation, He was crucified. Though the title above His cross read, "King of the Jews," Jesus has yet to rule as King.

At His trial, Jesus had told Pontius Pilate that His kingdom is not of this world system. Jesus will indeed someday assume His rightful place as "King of Kings" and "Lord of Lords."

This will occur when He comes again to rule the earth. It is then that the promise made to David, of the everlasting kingdom, will receive its complete fulfillment.

Was Jesus Always Confident
Of His Identity?

The Bible testifies that Jesus Christ is the eternal God who became a human being. He came to earth in order to sacrifice His life for the sins of the world. This brings up certain questions.

Was this something He was always aware of? Was there ever a time Jesus doubted His calling? Or, could it be possible that He was overwhelmed by all the attention that He received and allowed Himself to be taken for someone He was not? What does the evidence say?

HE WAS ALWAYS CONFIDENT OF HIS IDENTITY

The Bible is clear that Jesus was always confident of who He was, and why He had come to earth. From our first glimpse of Him, until the end of His life, we find Jesus confident of both His Person and His message. The evidence is as follows.

1. JESUS AT AGE TWELVE – HE WAS DOING THE WORK OF THE FATHER

The first encounter we have of Him, apart from the birth record, is at age twelve. Luke records the following.

> Every year his parents used to go to Jerusalem for the feast of the Passover. When he was twelve years old, they went up for the feast as usual. When the days of the feast were

over and they set off home, the boy Jesus stayed behind in Jerusalem without his parents knowing it. They assumed he was somewhere in the party, and it was only after a day's journey that they went to look for him among their relations and acquaintances. When they failed to find him they went back to Jerusalem looking for him everywhere. It happened that, three days later, they found him in the Temple, sitting among the teachers, listening to them, and asking them questions; and all those who heard him were astounded at his intelligence and his replies. They were overcome when they saw him, and his mother said to him, 'My child, why have you done this to us? See how worried your father and I have been, looking for you.' He replied, 'Why were you looking for me? Did you not know that I must be in my Father's house?' (Luke 2:41-49 NLT).

From this account, we see that at the age of twelve, Jesus knew of His identity. He told His mother Mary that He was in His Father's house. He reminded Mary who His real Father was. It was not Joseph—but rather God the Father.

As to exactly when and how He realized His identity we are not told. Scripture is silent on this matter. The only thing we can say for certain is that He did know His identity by the age of twelve. Apart from this, it is only futile speculation.

2. JESUS WAS ALWAYS CONFIDENT OF HIS IDENTITY DURING HIS PUBLIC MINISTRY

During Jesus' public ministry, His confidence in His calling was sure. The Lord told the religious rulers exactly where He came from.

You are from below; I am from above. You are of this world; I am not of this world (John 8:23 NIV).

Jesus clearly recognized His origin. He claimed to come from heaven above.

3. JESUS WAS CONFIDENT OF HIS IDENTITY AT THE GARDEN OF GETHSEMANE

If there ever were a time when one would expect Jesus Christ to have doubts about who He was, it would have been during His betrayal and death. But in the face of this great adversity, He never denied who He was, or the calling that He had.

In the Garden of Gethsemane, He was still confident of His identity as God's Son. Luke records Jesus' prayer.

> Then he withdrew from them about a stone's throw, knelt down, and prayed, "Father, if it is your will, take this cup {of suffering} away from me. However, your will must be done, not mine" (Luke 22:41,42 God's Word).

Jesus knew what He was about to face and He faced it with total trust in God the Father.

4. HE WAS CONFIDENT OF WHO HE WAS AT HIS TRIAL

At His trial, Jesus confessed to being the Christ. We read about the response of Jesus to the question of the High Priest.

> But Jesus remained silent. Then the high priest said to him, "I demand in the name of the living God that you tell us whether you are the Messiah, the Son of God." Jesus replied, "Yes, it is as you say. And in the future you will see me, the Son of Man, sitting at God's right hand in the place of power and coming back on the clouds of heaven" (Matthew 26:63,64 NLT).

Jesus realized that this confession would lead to His eventual death. If Jesus had any doubts about His calling, the trial was Jesus' chance to set the record straight. Yet Jesus made it clear that He believed Himself to be the Christ.

5. HE WAS CONFIDENT WHILE ON THE CROSS

Even when He was dying, Jesus was aware of His identity. He forgave the sins of a criminal that was dying next to Him. Luke records.

> Then he said, "Jesus, remember me when you come into your Kingdom." And Jesus replied, "I assure you, today you will be with me in paradise" (Luke 23:42,43 NLT).

Jesus was confident that He, along with this criminal, would be in paradise, namely heaven, upon their deaths.

Therefore, everything that we know about Jesus, from His early years through His death on the cross, tells us that He was always confident about His identity. He knew exactly who He was, and why He had come to this earth. He was the Lamb of God who would die for the sins of the world. There was never any doubt in His mind.

SUMMARY TO QUESTION 40
WAS JESUS ALWAYS CONFIDENT OF HIS IDENTITY?

As we study the four gospels, we find that Jesus Christ was always fully aware of His identity. From the age twelve, until His death on Calvary's cross, we find that Jesus was, at all times, certain of who He was, as well as why He was here upon the earth. Furthermore, He never once questioned His calling, or wavered on His identity. The evidence is as follows.

The first recorded words of Jesus are from an incident when He was twelve years of age. He became separated from His parents in the city of Jerusalem.

When they found Him three days later at the temple, the youthful Jesus was asking questions and giving answers which confounded the religious experts. Jesus then explained to Mary and Joseph that He had to be about His Father's business. This was not referring to Joseph—but rather to God the Father. Jesus was doing His work. Therefore, we discover that Jesus was aware of His calling at this early age.

This awareness continued throughout His life. During His public ministry Jesus taught that He was from heaven above. He was aware of His divine origin. This is something which He consistently taught.

At the Garden of Gethsemane, when He knew He was about to die, Jesus acknowledged His identity as well as His mission. At His trial, as well as upon the cross, the Bible also says that Jesus never wavered in acknowledging who He was, or why He had come to this earth.

As to when He became confident of who He was, the Bible does not tell us. What we can be certain of is this—from the age of twelve through the time of His death, Jesus was secure of His identity as God the Son.

Will Jesus Christ Have Two Natures Forever?

When God the Son came to this earth, He took upon Himself something which He had never had before—a human nature. Indeed, He was fully human as well as fully God. Furthermore, when Jesus came back from the dead He still had that human body—though it was a glorified one.

This brings up the question as to whether Jesus will be this way for all eternity. Will Jesus Christ have these two natures forever?

The Bible does seem to teach that two natures of Jesus Christ have become permanent. This can be observed by the following: Jesus' appearances after His resurrection, the promise at His ascension that the same Jesus would return, the description of Jesus after His ascension, the present role He has as our mediator, and the qualifications that are necessary for His High Priestly ministry. The New Testament says the following.

1. THE RESURRECTED CHRIST HAD A GENUINE BODY

The appearances of Jesus Christ after He came back from the dead showed that He still had a literal body. Luke testified that Jesus' body was missing from the tomb on Easter Sunday morning. He wrote.

And they entered in, and found not the body of the Lord Jesus (Luke 24:3 KJV).

His body was not there, but it was somewhere.

Matthew explains that certain women who came to the tomb, and found it empty, then met the resurrected Christ on their way back to the city.

And as they went, Jesus met them. "Greetings!" he said. And they ran to him, held his feet, and worshiped him (Matthew 28:9 NLT).

The body of Jesus was no longer in the tomb because He had risen. The fact that He could be held by the feet shows that Jesus had a genuine body.

Jesus Himself testified that He had an actual body after His death. He said the following to Mary Magdalene on the day of His resurrection.

Jesus said, "Do not hold on to me, for I have not yet ascended to the Father. Go instead to my brothers and tell them, 'I am ascending to my Father and your Father, to my God and your God'" (John 20:17 NIV).

Therefore, the risen Christ was not merely a spirit. Indeed, Jesus was raised in an actual body.

2. AT HIS ASCENSION THERE WAS A PROMISE OF HIS BODILY RETURN

At Jesus' ascension, there were certain angels who promised Jesus' disciples that He would return in the same manner in which He left this world. They said the following to the disciples of the Lord.

They said, "Men of Galilee, why do you stand looking up into heaven? This Jesus, who has been taken from you into heaven, will come in the same way that you have seen Him going into heaven" (Acts 1:11 HCSB).

Jesus left the earth as both God and man. Therefore, it seems necessary that Jesus remain the God-man until He returns.

Consequently, it seems that He will remain in that glorified body—at least until the time He returns as King of Kings.

3. JESUS APPEARED IN A BODY AFTER HIS ASCENSION

After His ascension into heaven, Jesus is still represented as having a body. When the martyr Stephen was being stoned to death he saw the risen Christ. He described Him as follows.

> "Look!" he said. "I see the heavens opened, and the Son of Man standing at the right hand of God (Acts 7:56 NET).

This is consistent with the risen Jesus still having a body.

4. HUMANITY IS NECESSARY FOR HIS ROLE AS HIGH PRIEST (INTERMEDIARY)

There is also the issue of Jesus mediating between God and humanity. The Apostle Paul told Timothy that the man, Christ Jesus, is interceding on our behalf.

> For there is one God and one intermediary between God and humanity, Christ Jesus, himself human (1 Timothy 2:5 NET).

It is the "human" Christ Jesus who is mediating for us. It seems that He must remain in that body to be our intermediary.

In fact, to be a High Priest, it seems that Jesus would have to remain human. Indeed, the Apostle Paul says that the same Jesus who died for us is also presently interceding for us. He wrote the following to the Romans.

> Who is the one who condemns? Christ Jesus is the One who died, but even more, has been raised; He also is at the right hand of God and intercedes for us (Romans 8:34 HCSB).

All of this seems to indicate the necessity that Jesus Christ remain in His glorified human body—at least through the time of His Second Coming to the earth.

After His Second Coming to the earth, there does not seem to be anything in Scripture which indicates, one way or the other, as to whether He will remain in that glorified form for all eternity. The Bible is silent on this matter.

SUMMARY TO QUESTION 41
WILL JESUS CHRIST HAVE TWO NATURES FOREVER?

God the Son, Jesus Christ, was fully God and fully human during the time when He was here upon the earth. Consequently, there is the issue with respect to the duration of the two natures of Jesus Christ. How long will He remain in this human form?

Scripture seems to teach that Jesus will retain His human nature forever—or at least through the time of His Second Coming to the earth. There are a number of reasons as to why this appears to be the case.

First, the resurrected Christ had a genuine body. In other words, He was not merely a spirit, a ghost. Scripture is clear on this issue. Jesus Christ was raised bodily from the dead.

The Bible also says the "same Jesus" that left the earth will return. Since Jesus left our world in a glorified body, it seems to follow that He will also return in that same glorified body. This indicates that He will remain in His glorified form—at least through the time of His Second Coming.

Also, the description of the Lord after His Ascension is consistent with one who has a body. When the martyr Stephen was dying, he saw Jesus standing at the right hand, or place of authority, of God the Father. This is also consistent with the idea that Jesus still resides in His glorified body.

In addition, the Apostle Paul said that the man Christ Jesus is our intermediary—the go-between between God and the human race. This is further indication that He remains in this glorified form.

Finally, it is necessary for Jesus' ministry as High Priest that He remains human. The High Priest is one who shares our nature and understands our feelings. Thus, it seems that Jesus must remain in that body as long as He is interceding for believers.

In sum, the Scripture teaches that God the Son, Jesus Christ, remains in the same body that was raised from the dead. We know that He will remain in that body through the time of His Second Coming to the earth. Beyond this, we can only speculate.

What Should We Conclude About The Identity Of Jesus Christ?

After looking at what the New Testament has to say about the Person of Jesus Christ, we can make a number of observations and conclusions about His identity.

1. JESUS WAS FULLY GOD

From the totality of Scripture, we find that Jesus Christ was fully God. The Bible says that He is the eternal God who has always existed, and always will exist. In fact, He is God the Son, the Second Person of the Holy Trinity. The Bible gives both direct and indirect evidence to this.

2. JESUS WAS FULLY HUMAN

Though Jesus was God the Son for all eternity, He became human at a certain point in history. Indeed, He came to a specific nation as a member of the human race. While He was supernaturally conceived, everything about His birth, childhood, and humanity was normal.

In other words, He was not super-human. Christ experienced all the things other human beings experience. This means that Jesus was human in every sense of the term.

Yet, there is one main difference between Jesus and the rest of us—He never sinned. Jesus went through His entire life without once breaking the laws of God. Therefore, while Jesus Christ was a human being, He was also perfect humanity.

3. THE INCARNATION IS A MYSTERY THAT WE CANNOT COMPLETELY UNDERSTAND

How God could become a human being with two natures, yet living in only One Person, is not completely understandable to us. God the Son becoming like one of us is certainly a mystery—a mystery the Bible does not attempt to explain.

Our responsibility is to accept what the Bible says about Jesus' deity as well as His humanity. In doing so, we must recognize that we will never fully understand this truth. It is important that we realize this.

4. JESUS IS PROPHET, PRIEST AND KING

Jesus Christ has three offices—Prophet, Priest, and King. When God the Son came to earth the first time, He came in the role of a prophet. He spoke God's truth to the people. However, His words were rejected. He was crucified on the cross of Calvary. His death on the cross was for the sins of the world. In other words, He died as our substitute.

Three days after His death on the cross, Jesus Christ rose from the dead. After appearing to certain people for some forty days, the risen Christ then ascended into heaven. Today, He intercedes for believers as our Great High Priest. He is the One through whom we pray. It is because of Jesus' role as our High Priest, that our prayers to God the Father are heard.

Jesus' coming to earth is not the last time the world will see Him. There will come a time when He will return to earth. When Jesus returns a second time, He will return as King. He will set up His everlasting kingdom that will have no end.

This is a brief summary of what the Bible says about the identity of Jesus. While there are many other things we would like to understand about Him, Scripture gives us sufficient information so that we can know who He is, what He has done on our behalf, as well as what He expects from us.

SUMMARY TO QUESTION 42
WHAT SHOULD WE CONCLUDE ABOUT THE IDENTITY OF JESUS CHRIST?

After looking at what the New Testament teaches about Jesus Christ, there are a number of observations and conclusions which we can make concerning who He is.

From the Bible, we find that Jesus Christ was fully God and fully human. He is the living God, God the Son, who became human at a certain time in history. Before He came to this earth He had only one nature—a divine nature. When He came to this earth He took upon Himself something which He did not previously have—a human nature.

While this is the teaching of Scripture, it is not totally understandable to us. In other words, it is a mystery as to how God could become a human. Our responsibility is not so much to understand this truth but rather to believe it.

Scripture also teaches that God the Son has three basic offices—that of a Prophet, Priest, and King.

Jesus Christ was a prophet, or a spokesman for God, at His First Coming. He spoke God's truth to the people. Unfortunately, His prophetic words were rejected. Instead of receiving Him as the Promised Messiah, they put Him to death. However, death could not hold Him. Jesus came back from the dead three days after His death. He rose from the dead in a glorified body never to die again.

Presently, Jesus Christ is our Great High Priest. This means that He is interceding for us to God the Father. It is because of Him, and what He has done, that we are able to have our prayers answered.

When Jesus returns to the earth, He will return as "King of Kings." At the time of His return, Jesus will set up His everlasting kingdom. He will remain King for all eternity.

This briefly sums up what the Bible says about the identity of Jesus Christ. Though we have many unanswered questions about Him, what the Scripture does tell us is certainly sufficient.

Our responsibility, therefore, is to learn what we can about Him and then act upon the things which we know are true. This is how we can live a life which is pleasing to Him.

About the Author

Don Stewart is a graduate of Biola University and Talbot Theological Seminary (with the highest honors).

Don is a best-selling and award-winning author having authored, or co-authored, over seventy books. This includes the best-selling *Answers to Tough Questions*, with Josh McDowell, as well as the award-winning book *Family Handbook of Christian Knowledge: The Bible*. His various writings have been translated into over thirty different languages and have sold over a million copies.

Don has traveled around the world proclaiming and defending the historic Christian faith. He has also taught both Hebrew and Greek at the undergraduate level and Greek at the graduate level.

Made in the USA
San Bernardino, CA
18 January 2020

63066008R00175